IRELAND

Land of Mist and Magic

by Kathleen Allan Meyer

Dillon Press, Inc.   Minneapolis, Minnesota 55415

Acknowledgments

The author gratefully acknowledges the assistance of the following individuals and organizations who expedited her research and/or supplied photographs for the text: Ruth A. Smith; Kathleen and Michéal Shivnan, Knockvicar, Ireland; Dymphna Regan, Knockvicar; Mr. and Mrs. John Burke, Knockvicar; Breeda Griffin, Lisdoonvarna, Ireland; Betty Kehelly, Calderwood House, Dublin, Ireland; Seamus O'Donnell, Ballyshannon, Donegal, Ireland; Mr. and Mrs. Noel McLoughlin, Galway, Ireland; Irish Tourist Board, Baggot Street Bridge, Dublin, Ireland—Noragh Owens, of "Meet the Irish" Publicity Department, and Margaret McGahon, Photo Officer/Librarian; Northern Ireland Tourist Board, River House, Belfast; Northern Ireland Tourist Board, New York; Irish Tourist Board, New York—Simon O'Hanlon, Rosaleen Carney; Irish Tourist Board, San Francisco—H.A. Gogarty, West Coast Regional Manager, Brigid Crowley, Teresa O'Carroll de Castillo; Thelma M. Doran, Consul General of Ireland, San Francisco, California; Dick Alexander, Travel Editor, San Francisco Examiner; John C. Broderick, Assistant Librarian for Research Studies, Library of Congress; Public Relations Department of Moore McCormack Resources, Inc., Stamford, Connecticut; Public Relations Department of Union Pacific Railroad Co., New York; Lensmen Limited, Lensmen House, Dublin; National Irish Library, Dublin; Mrs. Beatrice Shanahan; Noragh A. Smith; Molly Regan, children's librarian of the San Mateo, California, Public Library; the John F. Kennedy Library.

Library of Congress Cataloging in Publication Data

Meyer, Kathleen Allan.
    Ireland, land of mist and magic.

    (Discovering our heritage)
    Bibliography: p. 139
    Includes index.
    1. Ireland—Social life and customs—Juvenile literature.
2. Irish Americans—Juvenile literature.
I. Title. II. Series.
DA960.M48   1982   306'.09415   82-14668
ISBN 0-87518-228-3

Dillon Press, Inc., 242 Portland Avenue South
Minneapolis, Minnesota 55415

Printed in the United States of America
          4   5   6   7   8   88   87   86   85

Contents

Fast Facts About Ireland

Official Name: Republic of Ireland.

Capital: Dublin.

Location: North Atlantic Ocean; the Republic of Ireland occupies about five-sixths of the island of Ireland in the British Isles.

Area: 27,136 square miles (70,283 square kilometers); the greatest distances on the island of Ireland are 289 miles (465 kilometers) from north to south and 177 miles (285 kilometers) from east to west. Ireland has 1,738 miles (2,797 kilometers) of coastline.

Elevation: *Highest*—Carrauntoohill, 3,414 feet (1,041 meters) above sea level. *Lowest*—sea level along the coast.

Population: *Estimated 1982 Population*—3,519,000; *Distribution*—51 percent of people live in or near cities; 49 percent live in rural areas; *Density*—129 persons per square mile (50 persons per square kilometer).

Form of Government: Republic; *Head of Government*—prime minister.

Important Products: Barley, dairy products, livestock, potatoes; alcoholic beverages, chemicals, machinery, paper, processed foods, textiles.

Basic Unit of Money: Irish pound.

Major Languages: English and Gaelic.

Major Religions: Roman Catholicism and the Church of Ireland (Protestant).

Flag: Three broad, vertical stripes of green, white and orange.

National Anthem: "The Soldier's Song."

Major Holidays: Saint Brigid's Day—February 1; Saint Patrick's Day—March 17; Easter Day; Halloween—October 31; All Saint's Day—November 1; Christmas Day—December 25.

NORTH ATLANTIC OCEAN

SCOTLAND

NORTH CHANNEL

Giant's Causeway

DONEGAL

NORTHERN IRELAND

Mountains of Mayo

SLIGO

LEITRIM

MONAGHAN

ULSTER

Lough Neagh
Belfast

MAYO

CONNACHT

ROSCOMMON

CAVAN

IRISH SEA

Mountains of Connemara

LONGFORD

LOUTH

GALWAY
•Galway

WESTMEATH

MEATH

Galway Bay

ARAN ISLANDS

OFFALY

LEINSTER

DUBLIN

•Dublin

CLARE

LAOIGHIS

KILDARE

River Liffey

River Shannon

•Limerick

WICKLOW

LIMERICK

TIPPERARY

KILKENNY

CARLOW

REPUBLIC OF IRELAND

KERRY

MUNSTER

WEXFORD

Mountains of Kerry

Lakes of Killarney

WATERFORD

•Waterford

CORK

•Cork

NORTH AMERICA

EUROPE

ASIA

IRELAND

AFRICA

SOUTH AMERICA

AUSTRALIA

IRELAND
LEINSTER—Province
KILDARE—County
•Dublin—City

1. Gem of the North Atlantic

Think green! Now ten times that green! For Ireland is famous for its green farm and pasture lands. In fact, it may be the greenest country in the world.

Some call Ireland the "Emerald Isle" because its color reminds them of the bright green gemstone. Others use its Gaelic name, *Éire* (pronounced *AIR-uh*). Gaelic is the native Irish language.

Why is Ireland so green? The Irish say that their "soft" weather colors the land. Ocean winds bring frequent rains to this misty island in the North Atlantic just west of Great Britain. After the rain, which comes almost every day, bright sunshine brings a rainbow over the green-robed land.

In between rainbows and "raining cats and dogs," Ireland has a great deal of cloudy weather. The clouds keep the sun from drawing the rich color out of leaves and grasses. A mild climate also helps Ireland stay green summer and winter.

In the central part of the country, green pastures cover much of a gently rolling, lime-filled plain ringed by low mountains. The lime in the soil and the even rainfall make rich grasses for Ireland's cattle and famous horses.

*Peggy Munkdale of San Mateo, California, stands with Gil-
nocky Esmeralda, her Connemara pony. The Connemara
pony was first bred on Ireland's west coast in the early nine-
teenth century and is famous as a riding horse and show
jumper.*

Ireland is often called the land of the horse, and it ships them to all parts of the world. For many years they have won prizes in hunting, racing, and show-jumping, including many Olympic medals. Even Emperor Napoleon Bonaparte of France knew about Ireland's fine horses. Some say he brought his white charger, Marengo, from County Wexford in southern Ireland.

In the damp western part of the central plain are many peat bogs. These are swampy lands made up of dead plants and mosses that have built up over hundreds of years.

Turf, or peat, looks like wet, brown clumps of dirt. It is one of the country's most important resources. When it is dry, it makes a good fuel for fireplaces. The Irish have used it for heating and cooking since people first lived in Ireland. In rural areas today the blue puffs of smoke and the smell of the peat are still widespread.

There is no energy shortage in the homes of western and southern Ireland. In these areas many families rent strips of bog land from the owners and cut their own turf. The turf is cut into blocks in the spring with a spade called a *sleann*.

Since turf takes many days to dry, Irish engineers thought of ways to dry it faster. They invented floating machines that spread the peat into mud pies to

An Irishman cutting turf in County Galway.

harden. After the peat has hardened, other machines scratch it into a dust called milled peat. This dried dust can be burned as it is blown through big furnaces in power plants. One-fourth of Ireland's electricity comes from these turf power stations, which are run by the Peat Board of the Irish Republic. So much peat remains that it may last for centuries.

Peat bogs make up one-tenth of Ireland. The rest of the land is covered by mountains, meadows, pasture lands, steep ocean cliffs, lakes, and rivers. Ireland is about the size of the state of Maine.

Even though Ireland is a small country, it has 800 rivers and lakes. The lakes, called *loughs* (pronounced *lahks*), were formed thousands of years ago during the Great Ice Age. Ireland has the largest lake in the British Isles, Lough Neagh in Northern Ireland. It also has the largest river, the Shannon, which is 230 miles long and empties into the Atlantic Ocean on the west coast. The Shannon is an important inland waterway for shipping. Near Limerick its waters are used to produce Ireland's main source of electric power.

Ireland is divided into four provinces—Munster in the south, Leinster in the east, Connacht in the west, and Ulster in the north. They are often called Ireland's "Four Green Fields." The provinces are divided into thirty-two counties.

The northernmost province, Ulster, has nine counties. Six of these make up Northern Ireland, a part of the United Kingdom of Great Britain and Northern Ireland. The other three counties are in the Republic of Ireland, an independent country. The Irish Republic occupies five-sixths of the island of Ireland, and the remaining one-sixth forms Northern Ireland.

Many of Ireland's counties are known for something special. Antrim in the northeast has the Giant's Causeway, or Giant's Steppingstones. These ocean cliffs are made of lava—a melted rock from volcanic eruptions or cracks in the earth's surface—that cooled and hardened into strangely-shaped stones. An old legend tells that Finn MacCool, an Irish giant, built the roadway so that he could cross over to Scotland to fight another giant. The stones disappear under the North Channel between Northern Ireland and Scotland. Then they appear again on Staffa, a little Scottish island about twenty miles away.

In northwestern Ireland Donegal County has rocky mountains of granite along its coast. The mountains shelter green valleys with many small farms. Here the people have been known for centuries for their weaving and knitting, and parents today still teach these handicrafts to their children. Mountain sheep provide thick, strong wool for weaving fine

The Giant's Causeway in Antrim County, Northern Ireland.

Donegal tweeds. Another part of life in Donegal that hasn't changed is the use of Gaelic customs and language.

To the south of Donegal on the west coast is County Galway. Many of Galway's people also speak Gaelic and follow the old way of life. The Irish call an area like this one *Gaeltacht* (pronounced *gale-tac*). Few areas like it are left in Ireland today. Others can be found in northwest Mayo County and in some parts of counties Kerry, Cork, Waterford, and Meath.

The Connemara region in Galway is the largest Gaelic-speaking part of the country. Here, too, are traces of the Éire of long ago. On Saturday mornings old women in long, black shawls bring farm fresh eggs and vegetables to the market stalls in the towns. Donkey carts filled with peat or milk cans travel the roads past white, thatch-roofed cottages. Moving along with the carts are the tinkers, or travelers as they like to be called.

The tinkers have been traveling around Ireland for hundreds of years. In 1695 England passed the Penal Laws, which took away most rights of Irish Catholics. Catholic children were not allowed to go to school, and their parents could not own land. Without homes, the people began to live a wandering life in their wagons. Today several thousand tinkers still roam the backroads of their native land.

Now the tinkers travel in caravans and cars, but they still like to camp along the roadside. Each family returns to its own special campsite season after season. The tinkers hang their laundry out to dry on top of bushes and make themselves at home. Some litter the campsites, and farmers get upset.

The Irish government has tried to find homes for the tinkers in housing projects. Before long, though, they are off on the open road again, taking their children out of school. Tinker fathers make money by trading horses and selling scrap metal. They also send their small children out to beg. At one Dublin home, a ten-year-old Tinker girl returns each Thursday at noon begging for money. She has been coming there for five years.

Tinkers have a language all their own, and they have many beautiful blessings. One asks that "every hair on your head might turn into a candle to light your way to heaven."

Another Gaeltacht area is the Aran Islands in Galway Bay. Fewer than two thousand people live on these three rocky islands. Sturdy and hardworking, the islanders make their own soil by carrying baskets of sand and seaweed from the shore. Since harsh winds and rains wash away the soil, each year they must make more.

The people on the Arans lead a very simple life. Some still wear the costumes of long ago. In recent years, though, new ways of living have come to the islands. Modern little houses have begun to replace the old, thatch-roofed houses, and now homes and pubs have television and electricity. Young people can see movies and go to dances at the parish hall.

Fishing and cattle raising provide most of the jobs on the islands. Once only *currachs*, skin or canvas-covered boats, were used by the island fishermen. Today the islanders have a large, modern trawler fleet, too. Teenagers are trained to be skippers of the new ships.

Aran women and girls weave clothing and knit tams and sweaters. They use a special undyed wool, *bawneen*, that sheds rain. Besides being worn by the Aran fishermen, these sweaters are sold all over the world. For centuries the islanders have created beautiful patterns for knitting. Many years ago each family had its own design.

Unlike the Arans, the soil of the Irish midlands is rich and fertile. In this central plain, the climate is mild and ideal for dairy and livestock farming. Grass grows better here than farm crops, and the green pastures are filled with wildflowers and birds. The Irish have a saying about the birds that fly up from the land:

One for sorrow, two for joy,
Three to get married and four to die,
Five for silver, six for gold,
Seven for a secret never to be told.

The farms of the midlands are handed down from father to son and are worked by family members. Most of the farms are small, between thirty and fifty acres. The fields for crops and pastures for cattle are divided by hedges or stone walls. On market days the roads and squares are crowded with families driving cattle, sheep, and pigs to market. There is even a market for cattle to be shipped overseas near Phoenix Park in Dublin.

Dairy farmers sell their milk to creamery "coops." These enterprises are owned and operated by the farmers themselves. In the midlands it's not unusual to see large milk cans sitting at the crossroads waiting to be delivered to a creamery. Some cream will be made into butter, which is an important Irish export to Great Britain and other European countries.

In the midlands, too, the old way of life is changing. Young people are leaving the farms for work in the cities and sometimes for other countries. To encourage them to stay, the government is offering courses in all kinds of farming. A special school at Cork in southern Ireland offers young women training to teach these courses. The government is also finding ways for farmers to improve the grasses in their pastures. High quality grasses help to produce better beef cattle—another important Irish farm product and export.

In the southwest part of Ireland, a great number of young men and women have a different kind of work. Many factories owned by companies from other countries have been built in the cities of Limerick and Shannon in County Clare. The government of the Irish Republic has helped companies from all over the world to open new plants there. Today these factories provide jobs for thousands of workers.

Many young people from farms and towns come to the busy city of Dublin to find work in its offices, factories, and shops. Dublin is the capital and largest city of the Irish Republic. It is also the leading port. One of the city's chief exports is a dark beer called stout which is made at the Guinness Brewery. This world famous company has been brewing beer since 1759.

Dublin is located at the mouth of the River Liffey on the eastern coast. It has fine old buildings, open squares, and green parks. Phoenix Park is one of the largest in the world. Many of Dublin's parks and streets have been renamed after the Irish patriots who fought to free Ireland from English rule.

O'Connell Bridge and O'Connell Street run through the heart of downtown Dublin. The bridge spans the River Liffey.

Boys and girls in Dublin find many of the same
things to do as young people in North America.
They go to the movies, watch television, and eat
hamburgers at the local McDonald's. Those who are
interested in learning about Irish ways may visit the
many historic buildings and fine museums in the city.
Double-decker buses whiz past Dublin Castle and
two seven-hundred-year-old cathedrals. In the middle of this bustling city is Trinity College, which was
founded in 1591 by England's Queen Elizabeth. Five
thousand students from Ireland and other countries
study here.

Many of Dublin's people once lived on farms.
Because most come from country areas, Dubliners
are friendly and easy-going. They enjoy living here.
Their city is modern, and yet it often gives them the
feeling of living in a very big village.

One hundred miles north of Dublin is Belfast, the
capital of Northern Ireland and its chief port. There
are more factories in this area of Northern Ireland
than in the Irish Republic. Young men and women
from the farming towns come here to find jobs. Factories that make cloth, airplanes, and ships provide
most of the work. One of Belfast's most well-known
exports is fine Irish linen.

Belfast is also known as the "Cradle of the United
Irishmen Movement." This movement was formed in

1849 to free Ireland from English rule. In 1920 the British Parliament divided Ireland into two separate countries that were to remain part of Great Britain. Northern Ireland, with many English Protestants and few Catholics, accepted this plan. The Catholic majority in the rest of Ireland did not. Led by rebels called the Irish Republican Army (IRA), they fought for complete independence.

Later the southern Irish gained their freedom. They live in what is now known as the Republic of Ireland. Some of these Catholics still hope to force Great Britain to give up Northern Ireland. They believe that only then will the northern Catholics be treated fairly.

Since Ireland was divided, IRA raiders have attacked British soldiers and Protestants in Northern Ireland. During the 1970s and 80s, fierce fighting has raged in the streets of Belfast. Kidnappings and bombings have taken place. People, even children, on both sides have been killed. No one has yet found an answer to the "troubles" of today's Ireland.

While the fighting in Northern Ireland has been in the headlines, life in the Irish Republic has been changing for the better. There are more jobs than ever before for young men and women. Once many Irish had to travel overseas to find work. In recent years, though, some of these emigrants have returned to their homeland. In fact, more than twenty thousand Irish returned from abroad to live in the republic in 1979.

Irish education has also improved. Secondary schools are now open to all students, and many new schools for special training have been built.

The country areas young people are leaving behind are changing, too. Fewer fairs, donkey carts, and thatch-roofed cottages are there today than in the past. In a few years they will disappear from the narrow, stone-walled roads.

The Irish people, however, have not changed. They are and will be Ireland's greatest resource. Their courage, humor, imagination, and learning have deep roots in the past. These will be forever Ireland.

2. Those Who Are Irish

The Irish have a saying: "There are only two kinds of people—those who are Irish and those who want to be." This saying seems to be true on Saint Patrick's Day. Have you noticed that on this holiday people who aren't Irish wear green clothes, eat corned beef and cabbage, and sing Irish songs?

Who are the Irish? They aren't just one group of people. Invaders from many places came to live in Ireland. Each wave of invaders had different ways, and each looked very unlike the others.

Because of the different groups who came to Ireland, today's Irish don't look very much alike. To find out what their backgrounds are, let's imagine that we are walking down Dublin's O'Connell Street.

"Posting" a letter is a short, black-eyed Irishman with dark, curly hair. He is one of the Black Irish whose ancestors came from southern Europe.

A Foxy Irish has stopped at the Ironmonger's, or hardware store. He is of medium height and build and has blue eyes and red hair like the Vikings of Norway.

Standing by the store window is a tall, thin man from Northern Ireland. He looks as though he should be in a kilt, the skirt men wear in Scotland.

These Irishmen (above) *and the Irishwoman* (right) *have some of the features of the people who came to Ireland long ago.*

There are even more Irish to meet. The dark-haired, blue-eyed girl on the street corner may have grandparents in Galway because the Spanish settled there. And her blonde-haired friend with rosy cheeks inherited her features from still other people.

If we listen for a few minutes, we'll find the Irish don't sound alike, either. Those from southern Ireland have a pretty, musical voice. The people from Donegal speak in a rougher tone with a Scottish burr. And those from Northern Ireland have a British accent.

The people of the Irish Republic are proud of the old Gaelic language. Street and public signs are written first in Gaelic and then in English. Every student must learn the native language to qualify for jobs in government agencies. Today, however, most of the people speak English as their first language.

Expressing their Gaelic words in English has given the Irish a very special way of talking. If the weather is misty, they may say, "It's a fine, soft day." If it's pouring rain, they grumble, "This weather is enough to knock the top off your head!" And an Irishman who is pleased says, "That'll do me just grand." "Grand" is a word that the Irish often use.

For many things the Irish don't use the same English word that we do. The beach is the "strand." A policeman is a "garda." If the "geyser" (water heater) is broken, you'll be taking a cold shower. "Queue" at the movies to get your ticket. At a "sweet shop" (candy store), ask for a "mineral" instead of a soft drink.

Let's hope the car doesn't run out of "petrol" in the middle of Ireland's narrow roads. Car trouble means having to lift the "bonnet" (hood) and open the "boot" (trunk). If you're going to meet someone a week from today, the date is "this day week."

Irish names are more familiar because of the many Irish who live in North America. Many of the people have last names using two Irish words, *Mac* and *O*. *Mac* means "son of" and *O* "grandson." Long ago there were no last names in Ireland. When Brian Boru was high king of Ireland, just about everybody added Mac and O to their first name. King Brian's family became known as the O'Briens. Today the MacKennas, the MacFaddens, the MacNamaras, the O'Connors, the O'Kellys, the O'Hallorans, and all the rest of the O's and Mac's fill Irish telephone books.

Imagine what it would be like to have so many persons with the same last name in the telephone book. Then imagine the trouble you would have if the first names were the same, too. In Ireland that often happens. For most Irish babies are named after Ireland's saints, and there are only a limited number of saints' names to go around.

In western Ireland the Irish have solved this problem. Each Patrick O'Brien adds his father's name to his own. O'Brien letters are addressed to Patrick O'Brien John, Patrick O'Brien Michael, and so on.

Some Irish ways are similar to American ways, but not the Irish way of dealing with time. We're always in a hurry to keep an appointment or to get a project done. Most Irish are not. They never seem to mind being stopped for directions or for giving someone a hand. A recent visitor leaving an Irish town was looking for the right road. A tweed-caped Irishman, going the other way, turned his car about and led him safely out of town.

Business can wait, too. All banks and shops close for an hour or more in the middle of the day. If a visitor wants to cash a check or shop, he or she will just have to wait, relax, and talk!

"A word is more lasting than the wealth of the world," according to an old Irish saying. The Irish have always enjoyed talking and telling stories and jokes. They like to laugh and have others join with them, and they make jokes about themselves and their weather. Outside The Lobster Trap, a restaurant in Inishbofen, is a sign that says, "Menu—as changeable as the weather." The waitress might tell you that she is slow to serve you but quick to bring the bill.

Because the Irish enjoy talking to strangers, traveling is very pleasant in Ireland. A common sight in

An Irishwoman chats with a vendor on Moore Street in Dublin.

homes and inns is an old Gaelic saying, *céad mile fáilte*, which means "a hundred thousand welcomes." Part of the Irish welcome is sharing a cup of tea and a slice of delicious soda or oatmeal bread. In city or country, the kettle is always "on the boil." The Irish drink more tea than any other people except the English.

For the Irish singing is just one step away from talking. They have always been a musical people, perhaps because for centuries they had to find joy in simple things. Today they still like to sing.

Children learn Irish songs in the republic's schools. Many tell of "the troubles" during Ireland's fight for freedom from English rule. Some tell about the days when many Irish starved to death and others left their homeland. Songs are one way that children learn about the sad days of their country's history.

The Irish also take great joy in dancing. Long ago they danced in their homes or at the crossroads, and dances are still a favorite among teenagers and grown-ups. Today the old-time reels and jigs are danced all over Ireland in shows, festivals, and contests. In some schools the children are taught these dances in place of physical education classes.

If the Irish take anything more seriously than talking, singing, and dancing, it is religion. In the Republic of Ireland, nearly all the people belong to the Roman Catholic church. The Irish make their religion a part of everyday life. Crosses and holy pictures hang in the front windows and on the walls of their homes. Each day families kneel together and say a special prayer called the rosary. In schools there are many statues and pictures of the saints and the pope. As the bishop of Rome, the pope is the head of the Roman Catholic church all over the world.

From the time they are very small, Irish Catholic children attend a church service called mass on Sunday. For the Irish going to church is both a religious and social event. Parents and children are dressed in their best Sunday clothes. During the long service children are well behaved and quiet.

When mass is over, all the families gather outside to talk. "Please God" and "God willing" are phrases that are used often by the Irish. Instead of saying "Good-bye," they smile and say "God bless." A family from the parish usually invites the priest for Sunday dinner. Irish people respect him and what he believes in.

On feast days—special times in the Catholic year—priests lead many Irish on long walks to holy places. Croagh Patrick, Ireland's holy mountain, is one of the most famous. Catholics all over Ireland visit ancient holy wells in honor of the saints. The pilgrims come on the saints' feast days to pray and fill

The pilgrims (left) *are among the fifty thou-sand people who climb the slopes of Croagh Patrick, Ireland's holy mountain, each year on the last Sunday of July. Many climb barefoot during the night to arrive in time for a sunrise mass. The statue* (below) *is dedicated to Saint Patrick, who fasted on the holy mountain for forty days and nights.*

bottles of holy water to take home. They believe this water can cure people and animals who are ill.

The Irish not only respect their saints but also their scholars. Ireland was once known as the "Land of Saints and Scholars." Even though it is a small country, it has given the world many great writers and poets. Two of the most famous are James Joyce and W. B. Yeats. A fine poet, Yeats wrote a book of folk and fairy tales for children.

Jonathan Swift was an eighteenth-century Irish writer who wrote *Gulliver's Travels*, an exciting adventure story. Although he intended the story to be read by adults, young people enjoy it, too. The story tells of a ship's doctor who travels to an imaginary world called Lilliput where strange people only six inches high capture him. The Lilliputians have very silly laws in their kingdom. One is that everyone must break their eggs at the small end only. This law makes those who want to break them on the large end so angry that civil war breaks out. Swift points out in his book that people in our real world sometimes act just as foolishly as the Lilliputians.

Another early Irish writer was Oliver Goldsmith. He wrote one of the first children's books, *The History of Goody Two Shoes*. Before that time, books were written just for grown-ups, and children learned to read from adult books. Goldsmith also was one of the first writers to put all of the old nursery rhymes into one book. Most likely you learned some of these rhymes when you were small.

Maria Edgeworth, an author who lived a century after Jonathan Swift, is sometimes called the mother of children's literature. Maria started writing in an unusual way. As a young girl, she had to baby-sit her twenty-two brothers and sisters. She found she could keep them quiet by telling exciting stories with surprise endings. Her father helped her write them because he was interested in children's literature, too. The Edgeworths were among the first to publish books for children.

The most famous book in Ireland—the Book of Kells—was written hundreds of years before Maria Edgeworth began writing. Working by hand in monasteries, Catholic monks copied verses in Latin from the Bible and drew colorful pictures to go with them. These religious artists turned letters into artful animals and monsters. Written and painted in the eighth century, the Book of Kells is considered by some to be the most beautiful book ever made. The Irish keep it in the Trinity College library in Dublin. From time to time it is sent to museums all over the world so that others may enjoy it, too.

The Irish still make beautiful things today. One is tweed, which has been called "the cloth of kings"

This page from the Book of Kells shows how a Christian monk pictured Jesus more than a thousand years ago.

because it was first woven for Ireland's kings. Men and women weave the fine Irish tweed in the small cottages of Donegal. People the world over value this sturdy woolen fabric for its beauty and warmth.

We have seen that "those who are Irish" have some ways that are quite different from our own. Stories about the heroes, kings, and saints who walked the countryside of ancient Ireland help to show how these Irish ways came to be.

3. Heroes Old and New

Scientists who study the ways of life of ancient peoples have learned what we know about Ireland's first settlers. Campsites and shell mounds were made around eight thousand years ago by hunters and fishermen who came from mainland Europe.

About four thousand years later, Ireland's first farmers arrived. They grew wheat and barley and raised cattle, sheep, and pigs. At around the same time, black-haired, dark-skinned people came to Ireland by sea from Spain and Brittany. They used gold and bronze to make necklaces and swords, and they brought new beliefs and customs about the dead.

These people really believed in ghosts, goblins, and haunted houses. They thought the dead wandered about until the last night of the year, which for them was October 31. In America this night is celebrated as a time for spooky fun and games—Halloween.

Religious leaders called Druids taught the early Irish that gods and spirits lived in every lake, rock, and tree. The people built huge stone monuments to honor their gods. Some of these still stand in Irish pastures.

The Ireland of heroes and fierce battles began about 400 B.C. when Celtic tribes from Great Britain and northern France invaded the island. Their tall, blonde warriors fought with huge swords and shields. Often they bound themselves together with a chain so that they would fight until death came to them all. Before long, they gained control of all of Ireland.

The Celts liked to do more than just fight battles. They enjoyed hunting, dancing, telling stories, and reciting poetry, too.

At first they had no way of writing. Their poets, or *filids*, recited laws and legends from memory, and they were also the keepers of history. Later, each king kept a bard, or storyteller, at his court. The bard played on a harp and sang stories of his king's bravery in battle. Each Celtic family and its branches had a small kingdom known as a *tuath*, which was ruled by a *rí* or king. Only a wise and brave man was chosen to serve as a rí. He and his family lived on human-made islands called *crannogs* which were the beginnings of castles. At night the king's cattle stayed on the crannogs, too, because the kings liked to steal each other's cattle. Whoever had the most was said to be the richest.

A high king, or *árd-rí*, ruled over the other kings. His kingdom was at Tara, which is called the birthplace of the Irish nation.

Cormac MacArt was a lively árd-rí. Like all Irish kings, he placed his hand on the *Lia Fa'l*, the "Stone of Destiny," as he was crowned. According to legend, the stone sounded a mighty roar. Its noise could be heard by every one of the thousand guests in the great banquet hall, and all agreed that Cormac was the rightful king.

The kings of Munster had their own special place to be crowned. It was on top of a three-hundred-foot-high limestone rock jutting up from the flat plain of Tipperary. Irish legend tells how such a big rock ended up there. The devil took a big bite out of nearby mountains and spit it out in the middle of the plain. In the mountains is a space about the size of the rock.

Munster's king, Corc, called it Cashel, or the "rock of tribute." He decided to build a fine palace on it after hearing a strange tale from two pig herders. The herders had seen a vision as bright as the sun near the bare rock. In their vision a figure blessed the hill and said that a holy man named Patrick would soon come to Ireland.

Niall of the Nine Hostages, a high king, made this promise come true. Like all Celts, Niall enjoyed a good fight. When things got dull, he raided Britain to capture slaves. On one of these raids, Niall kidnapped a Roman boy called Patrick and sold him to a chieftain in Ulster. Young Patrick was put to work tending

An aerial view of the Rock of Cashel. The kings of Munster were crowned here in front of the cross of Saint Patrick.

sheep. After six years of slavery, he escaped by sneaking aboard a ship sailing for France.

Some years later, when Patrick was safely home in Britain, he had a dream. In the dream he was reading a letter from Ireland that contained a startling message: "We ask thee, boy, come and walk among us once more." Patrick believed that the dream was a call from God for him to go back to Ireland and spread the Christian faith there.

When he returned, many of the people did not believe in him and his God. Like the earlier Irish, the Celts believed in the Druid gods. Dichu, an Irish chief, was one of those who followed the Druid religion. One day he saw a group of strangers coming towards his home. He picked up his sword and shield and called his savage hunting dog. One brave man kept coming towards him. When Patrick spoke kindly to Dichu's dog, it stopped snarling and licked his hand.

Dichu welcomed Patrick into his home. Patrick taught the Irish chief the Christian religion and baptized him. Dichu gave him one of his barns, which became Patrick's first church in Ireland.

Many stories have been told about Patrick and the miracles he performed. One of the legends shows how strong his faith was.

Before the people would accept his God, Patrick had to prove that his faith was stronger than that of the chief Druid. The two leaders agreed to a test of skills. First, the Druid spoke magic words, and the plain below the castle became covered with deep snow. Patrick asked him to remove the snow. The Druid used all his magic but could not. Then Patrick blessed the plain, and the snow vanished. Next, the Druid caused a great darkness to fall around them. Patrick prayed, and the darkness became light. From that time on, the high king of Tara allowed Patrick to preach throughout the kingdom.

Patrick baptized many Irish and had churches built for these new Christians. He had a more lasting effect than any later invader. In time he became the patron saint of Ireland, and today Irish all over the world honor him on Saint Patrick's Day, March 17.

The Saint Patrick's Day parade in Dublin.

Patrick opened many monasteries for the religious training of Christian men. Women had their religious centers, too. Saint Brigid, honored by today's Irish, was the leader of one of them. Writers and artists came to Irish monasteries from all over the world. During the time Patrick preached in Ireland, wild, savage tribes from northern Europe attacked the Roman Empire. The period after Rome was conquered in A.D. 476 is known as the Dark Ages. Many of the Roman monks and scholars fled to Ireland. They brought books, gold, and precious stones.

In a land far to the north, now known as Scandinavia, the Vikings learned of Ireland's treasures. About A.D. 795 these fierce seafaring raiders set sail in ships with dragonheads at their bows. They wore coats of metal and carried flashing swords. Arriving on the south and east coasts of Ireland, they beheaded monks and nuns. Children were taken as slaves and put into the raiders' ships. The Vikings carried off gold and jewels and burned manuscripts. Before leaving, they set fire to churches and monasteries.

After many Viking raids, the Irish thought of a way to protect themselves. They built round towers more than one hundred feet high. At the sound of a warning bell, they grabbed books and valuables. Then they climbed up a ladder to a narrow doorway in a tower fifteen feet above ground, and the ladder was pulled up after them. Long, cold hours passed before the enemy left.

For more than two hundred years, the Irish put up with the Viking raids. Finally they began to live together in walled settlements and use the Vikings' weapons.

In 1002 Brian Boru became high king of Ireland. He organized the leaders of several Irish kingdoms into a strong union with a well-trained army. In a great battle in 1014 at Clontarf, now part of Dublin, the Irish army defeated the Vikings.

After their defeat, many Vikings sailed for home. Others were allowed to stay in the seaport towns they had founded—now known as Cork, Dublin, Limerick, and Waterford. More than one hundred years later, they helped the Irish fight the next invaders— the Normans.

The trouble started when an Irish king went to Britain for help because he had lost his kingdom. The Norman king of England, Henry II, sent the Earl of Pembroke, a nobleman, back with him. Nicknamed "Strongbow," he was known for his bravery. His knights wore shining armor and used bows and arrows. They battered down town walls with long logs and giant catapults, devices that could launch large rocks into the air. The Irish, who used only swords and axes, were no match for this new enemy.

By the 1300s, the Normans held nearly all of Ireland. As time passed, however, many Normans began to dress, act, and think like the Irish. Since the English kings didn't want to lose their power, they passed the Laws of Kilkenny. These harsh laws punished both the Irish and the Normans. The Irish were forbidden to use their native language or Irish names. The Normans were ordered not to marry the Irish, ride a horse Irish style without a saddle, play Irish games, or invite an Irish poet or musician into their homes. The Laws of Kilkenny made the Irish angry. Secretly, they kept their language, folktales, and legends alive through the *seanchais*, or wandering storytellers.

For centuries the Irish suffered under English rule. In 1541 Henry VIII, the king of England, forced Ireland's parliament to declare him king of Ireland. He told Catholics they must obey him instead of the pope. His daughter, Mary I, began what is known as the "plantation" of Ireland. She seized the land of the Norman noblemen and gave it to English settlers. Another daughter, Elizabeth I, outlawed Catholic church services and ordered the hanging of a number of bishops and priests. Despite the danger to their safety, priests continued to hold mass in secret.

One hundred years after Henry VIII declared himself king of Ireland, the Irish rose up against

English rule. Oliver Cromwell, a stern English leader, decided to crush the Irish Catholics once and for all. In one raid, called "Cromwell's Curse," his soldiers killed hundreds of men, women, and children. Cromwell had small children shipped as slaves to the West Indies and the American colonies. By making the Catholics suffer, the English rulers hoped to force them to leave Ireland. Instead, the Irish became more determined than ever to stay in their misty homeland.

The Irish struggle for freedom from England took a new turn when some Protestants formed the United Irishmen to seek equal rights for all the Irish people. Wolfe Tone, a young Protestant lawyer, was one of the leaders who joined forces with the Catholics. In 1798 he secretly went to France to get help. The French supplied him with 15,000 soldiers and 43 ships to invade Ireland. High winds kept Tone's force from landing on its first attempt, but a few months later he tried again. This time the English discovered the French fleet and captured Tone. Before he could be hanged, he killed himself.

The spirited Irish rebels began to worry the English Parliament. In 1801, under the Act of Union, lawmakers made Ireland part of the United Kingdom of Great Britain and Ireland. The Irish no longer had a parliament, and Catholics were not allowed to represent Ireland in the English one.

Then a new leader emerged to champion the rights of the Irish people. As a boy, Daniel O'Connell learned Gaelic and listened to the old tales. He was told that Cromwell's soldiers had driven his ancestors from their land. Later, as a young Catholic lawyer, he saw the English flag raised over Dublin Castle.

O'Connell vowed to free his country without any fighting. He asked the small parish churches to send pennies for his cause, and he used this money to buy newspaper ads. In 1829 he helped to pass the Catholic Emancipation Act. This act removed many of the laws that made life hard for Catholics. Now they could serve in the British Parliament and hold other public offices.

Despite their newly gained rights, most Irish Catholics were still poor farmers who lived on small plots of land. In 1845 a plant disease attacked the potato, Ireland's main food. Without enough to eat, 750,000 people starved to death or died from disease. Hundreds of thousands more left for Britain, the United States, and Canada. The British government passed new laws to help the Irish farmers. Many Irish, however, had suffered greatly under British rule. They wanted freedom.

On Easter Monday 1916, patriots from a group called the Irish Republican Brotherhood seized government offices in Dublin. After five days of fighting, the Irish rebels held only the post office. Then it caught on fire. Padraic Pearse, their leader, asked his men to surrender. Soon afterward, he and many of the republican leaders were shot to death by a British firing squad. Other rebels were sent to prison.

One of the leaders who was put in prison was Eamon de Valera. Three years later, he and his followers formed an Irish parliament called *Dáil Éireann* and declared all Ireland an independent republic. The British sent in soldiers and special police. Fighting broke out between them and a newly-formed Catholic group, the Irish Republican Army (IRA). For two years people were killed and homes burned. At last, in 1921, the Irish rebels and Great Britain agreed to a treaty that made southern Ireland the Irish Free State. Most of Ulster, or Northern Ireland, voted to remain part of Great Britain.

One group of Irish, led by Eamon de Valera, wanted all of Ireland to be free from British rule. A civil war broke out between this group and the Irish who accepted the division of their island. Later De Valera formed a new political party called the *Fianna Fáil* whose name honored the heroes of early Irish legends. After he was elected prime minister, the Irish Parliament wrote a new constitution for their country. The name of the king of England was left out of it, and Ireland's name was changed to Éire.

Eamon de Valera, a leader of the 1916 Easter Uprising and later prime minister of the Republic of Ireland.

In 1949 southern Ireland finally cut all its ties with Great Britain. The Irish Free State became the independent Republic of Ireland. Irish republicans wanted Northern Ireland to become part of the republic, and armed IRA members often raided Ulster.

Twenty years later a civil war broke out between Protestants and Catholics in Northern Ireland. The fighting is still going on today. Again and again, IRA raiders have attacked Protestants and British soldiers. They have staged bombings and kidnappings in England as well as in Northern Ireland. Protestants have attacked and killed many Catholics, too.

In 1976 two Catholic women, Mairead Corrigan and Betty Williams, quietly formed a group called Women for Peace in Belfast. They hoped to bring Catholics and Protestants together to stop the terrible fighting. In one month the brave women gained thirty thousand supporters of both religions and led "peace walks" into fighting zones. They asked all groups to hand in their weapons, and they arranged escapes for both Catholics and Protestants on blacklists. For their actions the women received death threats, were beaten, and had their cars smashed. People all over the world supported them. In 1977 Mairead Corrigan and Betty Williams won the Nobel Peace Prize for their efforts to bring peace to a troubled land.

Still, the fighting goes on. Since 1969 more than two thousand people have been killed. One of the recent victims was Lord Louis Mountbatten of the British royal family. After hundreds of years of "troubles," peace does not come easily.

In the last few years, sports teams and choirs

from Northern Ireland and the republic have visited each other. These contests have been peaceful. The Irish joy in sports and singing was the common bond between the people of the north and south.

Bringing together Catholic and Protestant teenagers could be another step toward peace. In Northern Ireland many workshops have opened for these young people. Here they learn to get along and accept each other's points of view. The government of Northern Ireland has donated money for these workshops. In the United States a group of Irish Americans called The Ireland Fund has raised more than half a million dollars to help the work for peace.

Peace has not yet come to Ireland, but progress has. The Irish in the republic now have a richer and more secure way of life. With many countries buying Ireland's products, more money is coming into the country. Life is no longer as hard as it was under British rule. More food is on the table, the schools are better, and all over the lovely, green countryside small, modern stone houses spring up near old, thatch-roofed cottages. The sacrifices of the past have brought freedom and opportunity to the Irish of today.

4. Of Leprechauns and the Blarney Stone

It's round as an apple,
As deep as a cup,
And all the men in Ireland
Could not lift it up!

Can you guess the answer to this riddle? Children in Ireland have heard it many times. Quickly they will answer, "A well!"

The Irish enjoy riddles, jokes, and sayings, and they have been telling some of them for hundreds of years. Many of the old sayings have come across the ocean with Irish immigrants to North America.

Perhaps your parents have said, "You are as busy as a bee." When you are too sure something good will happen, they may say, "Don't count your chickens before they are hatched." And when they want you to do something right now, you may hear, "Never put off 'til tomorrow what you can do today." These are all old Irish sayings.

When we speak of the month of March, we sometimes say that it came "In like a lion and out like a lamb." Many brides wear four things for good luck:

Something old,
Something new,
Something borrowed,
Something blue.

These are old Irish sayings, too.

Not all of today's Irish believe in the stories that have been passed down from past generations. Many people in rural areas, though, still do. They have faith in the saying that a donkey's shoe brings good luck. If one is found, it is nailed to the doorpost to guard a home. The Irish are very fond of their donkeys because the Bible says that one was present at Christ's birth.

Some country people believe that having tiny elves called leprechauns near their home brings bad luck. According to Irish folklore, these small fairies are real mischief-makers. Leprechauns don't like pointed fence posts, though. Many fences in the countryside were built this way to keep these nosy creatures from getting into trouble.

Even though leprechauns bring bad luck, most of the Irish who believe in them would like to meet one. The leprechaun is the shoemaker for the fairies. He is also the richest of them all, for he is their banker and stores their gold in a crock. His crock is found at the

This charming Irish couple, the Shivnans, have a donkey's shoe on their door for good luck.

end of rainbows. You can imagine why this tiny old man is not too fond of Ireland's frequent rainstorms. No matter how fast he moves his treasure, he can't escape the fast-moving rainbows!

Have you ever wanted to catch a leprechaun? Some Irish will tell you how. Look him in the eye, and then ask for his gold. If you keep your eye on him, he never refuses. Watch out, though, because he will think of ways to make you turn your head. Slipping away like a greased pig, he is gone forever!

One Irish folktale tells about a boy named Pat who caught a leprechaun. Seeing Pat's hard gaze on him, the little elf said, "Follow me. I'll lead you to my pot of gold."

He led poor Pat on a merry chase over bog and hill. Then he pointed to a bush. "Dig there!" he cried.

"I'll run home for a spade," replied Pat. "Don't move." But first he tied a red scarf on the bush to mark it. Quick as a wink, he was back. The leprechaun had vanished, and every bush in the field was tied with a red scarf!

The *far darrig*, or red man, is another mischievous elf. This little fairy has red hair, a red nose, and a red cap and coat. In winter he lives on someone's hearth and steals a smoke from filled pipes. He enjoys playing jokes on children who do not obey.

Unlike the leprechaun and the far darrig, the

púca travels alone in the dark. He can change himself into a frightening black horse. Legend says that Brian Boru tamed the púca with a bridle made out of three hairs from its tail. At the first pull, the hairs turned into bands of steel. The púca fainted, and Brian Boru revived it. Blessing himself, Ireland's high king made the púca promise never to kill anyone again—except those who aren't Irish.

Some púcas disguise themselves as snails. When Irish children see a snail, they will often sing, "Púca, púca, put out your horns."

A *banshee* is a scary fairy woman with a high wailing voice. Long ago, in the ruling Irish families, she would tell when death was coming. It is said that in ancient Ireland the banshee rode into battle with the warriors of these families. She shrieked to encourage them to fight harder.

"Trooping" fairies like to be together. Most live in merry bands in *raths*, or fairy forts. These are small mounds of dirt enclosed by a ring of trees or rocks. Some Irish say that there are more than thirty thousand raths in Ireland, all guarded by yellow gorse hedges and overgrown fuchsia. A story is told that one of these earth rings was found when workmen were laying out Shannon Airport in 1969. No Irishman would take part in digging it up. Englishmen were found to do the job.

No one knows for sure how the fairies came to Ireland. Some Irish believe they are the Druid gods who lived in every tree, lake, and rock. Those who believe in fairies say that they can be kind to people or play tricks on them. Their tricks include destroying farmers' seeds, breaking eggs, and kicking over milk pails. According to one saying, a restless horse has a fairy on its back. "God bless you" is often said in Ireland when someone sneezes. This blessing started long ago when people thought fairies made them sneeze and trip over things. Saying the blessing, the Irish believed, broke the spell.

Irish bookstores have many fairy tales in which these magical creatures play an important part. Sinéad de Valera, the wife of Eamon de Valera, the Irish patriot and prime minister, wrote several of them. One of her best stories is called *The Fairies Revenge.*

It is the story of Conn and Nuala, a young brother and sister. Near their home are mounds which are said to be fairy dwellings. Warned by their parents not to go "where the good people live," Nuala disobeys. She picks pretty white violets near the fairy ring and places them beside her bed. That night they disappear.

When Nuala goes to lie down, she finds sharp thorns in her bed. As fast as her parents take them out, they reappear. The family realizes that she is under a fairy spell for taking the fairies' flowers. Sorcha, a *bean feasa* or an old woman with magic powers, tells them they must do something to please the fairies and break the spell. She says that the fairies love to dance and suggests that Conn could whistle for them.

That night Conn sneaks out to the fairy ring and learns the fairies' tunes. The fairy queen is so pleased that he is able to play for their dancing that she grants him a wish. Conn asks for Nuala's spell to be broken.

The queen tells him to go to the mountain where the black witch lives. There, while the witch is sleeping, he must gather the leaves of the bittersweet plant. Then he must place these leaves in his sister's bed. Only then will she be able to sleep peacefully again.

As Conn is gathering the leaves, the witch awakens. She chases him as he flees down the mountain. Since Conn has rubbed his bare feet on a magic flat stone, he is able to escape. That night he places the leaves in Nuala's bed. The thorns disappear, and his sister is able to sleep in her bed once more.

The Irish enjoy their legends as well as fairy tales. Many of the legends are stories about the deeds of ancient Ireland's heroes. One of the cycles, which is a group of related tales, tells about Ulster's heroes. The most famous was the boy hero, Cuchulainn. He had even more magical powers than Superman. With this magic he was able to recapture Ulster's magical brown bull, Donn Cuailnge, from Queen Maeve of Connacht.

In battle Cuchulainn could change himself into a savage dragon shape, and he wore an invisible cloak that protected him from all harm. A crested war helmet on his head let out horrible cries to frighten the enemy. Circling his helmet were goblins, demons, and spirits that gave out savage shrieks. A beam of light as bright as ten torches shone from his forehead. In one hand he held ten enemy heads, and in the other he grasped nine more. Fighting alone, Cuchulainn could slay thousands of soldiers.

Maildun was another early Irish hero who had many strange and exciting adventures. When his father was slain, the Druid Naca told him to build a curragh to search for his father's murderers. The boat, said Naca, must have a crew of exactly sixty men.

After Maildun had chosen his crew of sixty, his three brothers climbed aboard. Then bad luck came to them all. For years they drifted from island to island. Many times they were almost killed. They met people-eating ants, a herd of red-hot pigs, and a huge animal with legs like a dog, teeth like a saw, and great sharp blue claws. On other islands they were chased by giants, a sea serpent, and a cat that turned itself into a blazing fiery arrow. Maildun and his crew thought they would never see Ireland again.

Many years later, they saw a tall silver pillar rising from the sea. A shiny silver net hung down from the top. Duiran, one of the crew members, cut off a small piece to carry home as an offering to the church.

Finally, on a distant islet, the Irish adventurers met a holy hermit. He told them they would reach Ireland safely. On the way, he said, they would find the man who killed Maildun's father. The hermit advised Maildun to forgive the murderer, for God had brought him safely through many dangers during his travels. Maildun followed his advice. When the crew finally arrived in Ireland, they found their families waiting for them. Duiran kept his promise, too, when he hung the piece from the silver net on the high altar of Armagh.

Like Maildun, Saint Brendan, the Navigator, sailed in a curragh to many faraway places. He went, though, for a different reason—to spread the Christian religion.

One ancient writing says that this Irish monk traveled to North America nine hundred years before Christopher Columbus. No one knows if Saint Brendan actually made this journey. But in 1976 the

Brendan, a thirty-six-foot curragh, sailed from Ireland to North America to prove that such a trip was possible. The boat is now on display at the Craggaunowen Project in County Clare.

The legend of the blarney stone is one of the favorite tales about Ireland's many castles. Centuries ago, Queen Elizabeth I asked Cormac MacDermod, lord of Blarney Castle, to prove he was loyal to her by giving away his castle. He agreed, but each time she asked him to give away the castle, he had an excuse for not doing it. At last the queen grew tired of all the excuses. When she heard yet another one, she said, "More Blarney talk!" To this day blarney is called the secret weapon of the Irish.

Dunguaire Castle in Galway is known for the legend of the Road of the Dishes. Long ago King Guaire was the master of this castle. He was called "Guaire, the Generous," because his right arm was longer than his left from giving away so much gold to the poor. One day the king was entertaining guests at a fine banquet. He blessed the meal, and then he added these words: "If anyone in my kingdom is more worthy of such a meal than we, it is my earnest wish that he receive it." No sooner had the words left his lips than the tablecloth, dishes, and food flew away through the air. King Guaire ordered his horses so that he could follow them.

Blarney Castle in County Cork.

Now near the castle lived a young monk and a holy man called Colman. They had just sat down to their plain meal of bread, an egg, and a mug of water. The young monk grumbled about the lack of food. Colman told him that God would provide a meal worthy of their holiness.

Suddenly the dishes, tablecloth, and food came flying through the air. Though Colman and the monk were surprised, they thanked God for the unexpected gift and began eating the fine feast. Soon they heard horses coming down the road. The monk was afraid, but Colman said no harm would come to them. At that moment the hooves of the king's horses stuck to the road. They did not move again until Colman and the monk had eaten their fill.

Impressed by the strange happenings, King Guaire got off his horse. He thought that Colman must be a very holy man indeed, and he asked him to serve as the bishop of all his lands. Colman was able to build a fine church on that spot. Later he was made a patron saint of this area of Ireland. Today there is a road called the Road of the Dishes leading from the castle to the place where Colman's church was built.

Like Irish legends, the folktales of Ireland have been passed down from generation to generation. For centuries these tales about country people existed only in the memories of the seanchais.

One folktale tells the story of Hudden, Dudden, and Donald O'Nery, three neighbors. Hudden and Dudden were jealous of Donald O'Nery. They decided to kill his bull so that he would be forced to sell his land to them.

When poor Donald discovered his dead bull, he took its hide to town to sell it. On the way he found a talking bird called a magpie. Through a bit of a trick, Donald made an old woman think the magpie was magical. She gave him a hatful of silver for it. Before long Hudden and Dudden saw the silver. When Donald told them that he had received it for the hide, they decided to kill their bulls, too. Of course, they were paid very little for the hides.

After Donald had played a few more tricks on Hudden and Dudden, they decided to get rid of him once and for all. They put him in a sack and started for the river. Along the way they ran off to chase a rabbit. Donald, who was tied in the sack, began to sing very happily. A cattle drover passing by asked him why he was singing.

"Oh, I am going to heaven, and I'll have no more troubles," replied Donald. The drover offered him twenty head of fine cattle if he could take his place in the sack. Donald agreed and tied him up. Then he drove the heifers home. When Hudden and Dudden returned, they drowned the drover instead of Donald.

Arriving home, they were surprised to find Donald alive and with such a fine herd. Donald told them that there were many more cattle under the water where they had come from. He even offered to show them the spot.

At the river Hudden jumped in first. As he drowned, he made a bubbling sound.

"What is that he is saying now?" asked Dudden.

"Faith, he is calling for help, there are so many cattle to bring up," replied Donald O'Nery. "I think I best leap in to help him."

Greedy Dudden pushed him aside and jumped in.

And that was the end of Hudden and Dudden!

5. Around the Irish Year

First Footing Day, Puck's Fair, Little Christmas—
these are special days on an Irish child's calendar. The
Irish have so many holidays and festivals that it
almost seems as if there were one for every day! Most
of them honor the church or celebrate important
farming days as they did long ago.

Old Irish customs are still an important part of
these holidays and festivals. First Footing Day comes
on January 1. People from Antrim in the north to
Cork in the south take part in this tradition.

The Irish believe that on January 1 the first foot
inside the house brings the kind of luck a person will
have all year. To have good luck, the first visitor
should:

Be a dark-haired boy or man, handsome and
   healthy;
Arrive a minute or two past midnight;
Bring a gift of either coal, bread, or silver coins,
And something to drink.

A red-haired girl or woman should stay away. She
would bring bad luck at that hour.

On January 6 children celebrate Epiphany, or Little Christmas. For the Irish this day marks the end of the Christmas season. Twelve candles are lit in many homes for the twelve disciples, the men who according to the Bible were sent out by Christ to teach in his name. Children look forward to Little Christmas because their mothers bake special cookies and cakes to eat at teatime.

Next comes Saint Brigid's Day on February 1, a church festival and school holiday. Saint Brigid was once a cowherd. She had such a great love for the land that she took part in tending the crops and caring for the cattle.

Schoolchildren learn the legend about Saint Brigid's cross. One day Brigid came to the home of a dying chieftain. As she sat beside him, she picked up some rushes from the floor and used them to make a cross for him. She told him about the meaning of the cross in her Christian religion. From that time on, Irish people have made crosses like hers out of rushes and have placed them in fields and barns to bring good luck.

Today, on the eve of this celebration, children still pull the rushes by hand and make crosses to hang in their homes and barns. Even the Irish television service honors Saint Brigid. It has adopted her cross as its emblem.

These Irish schoolchildren are making Saint Brigid's Day crosses out of rushes.

Not long after Saint Brigid's Day, Lent begins. For Irish Christians these forty weekdays before Easter are the most important religious time of the year. On the eve of Lent, Shrove Tuesday, most families follow the old custom of eating pancakes. Many years ago the Irish fasted, or ate very little, during Lent. Since in those days flour could not be stored for weeks, it was used up by making pancakes.

The day after Shrove Tuesday is known as Ash Wednesday. Parents and children attend special church services where priests place ashes on their foreheads in the shape of a cross. The cross is a sign that the worshipers regret their sins. In some country churches the people bring their own ashes to be blessed.

During Lent, on March 17, the Irish celebrate their greatest feast day of all—Saint Patrick's Day. Early in the day families fill the churches. Afterward many Irish march in long parades led by fife and drum bands. In country areas children wear shamrocks which they have gathered from the fields. Legend says that Saint Patrick picked up a shamrock at the Rock of Cashel to explain some of his teachings. The shamrock has been a religious symbol for the Irish ever since.

The largest Saint Patrick's Day parade is held in Dublin. It is reviewed by the lord mayor of the city from a grandstand on O'Connell Street. The mayor opens the parade by riding at its head in a fancy gold coach. As many as six bands have come from North America for the parades in Dublin, Galway, and Limerick. Bands also come from France, Germany, Finland, Switzerland, Great Britain, and even from wartorn Northern Ireland. Saint Patrick's Day is so important to Dubliners that they celebrate it for an entire week.

Irish children enjoy marching in Dublin's Saint Patrick's Day parade.

The town of Waterford has started a new Saint Patrick's Day tradition. The Irish ambassador in Washington, D.C., presents the president of the United States with a Waterford crystal bowl filled with shamrocks.

Americans enjoy honoring Saint Patrick, too. The first Saint Patrick's Day parade was held in New York City in 1779 to the tune of the fife and drum. It was attended by Irish soldiers of the British Army, which was occupying the city at the time. Today Irish Americans march down Fifth Avenue past Saint Patrick's Cathedral. Parades are also held in eight other American cities.

Two weeks after Saint Patrick's Day, the Irish celebrate a lighthearted holiday. April Fools' Day had its beginnings in the old Irish custom of giving someone a letter to deliver. The letter said, "Send the fool farther." Then the person who received it would put the message in another envelope and send it on to someone else. The poor person who delivered the message kept going from place to place.

The Sunday before Easter, Palm Sunday, is an important church festival. Irish families go to church and receive palm branches that have been blessed by the priests. After church the children make little crosses out of pieces of palm in memory of Jesus' sacrifice on the cross.

As Lent draws to an end, families attend church on Good Friday for three hours. For Irish Catholics this time represents the hours Christ hung on the cross. Even today no cakes are baked on this day without placing the sign of the cross on them.

Easter is a joyful day for Christians everywhere, for they believe that almost two thousand years ago Christ rose from the dead on this day. In Ireland

Easter and eggs have always been thought of together. Eggs are a symbol of the beginning of life. Years ago a popular Easter present among country people was a *cluideog* (about a dozen) of eggs.

Irish children do not get Easter baskets. Instead, they boil eggs and decorate them. Then they have a contest to see who can eat the most eggs.

When spring comes, the Irish may greet a visitor with "You're as welcome as the flowers in May." This old saying comes from an ancient country festival which is now called May Day. Long ago the Druids celebrated this day in honor of the fire and sun god, Baal.

In early Christian times children gathered branches of primroses on May Day. They laid them on doorsteps and window sills and placed them in barns to protect their houses, farm animals, and crops from mischievous fairies.

Today children still follow the custom of spreading primroses at the door on the first day in May. They also make posies, or small bouquets. The young people leave their flowers in honor of Our Lady, Saint Mary, for May is her special month.

The beginning of summer brings Midsummer Eve, a night of fun and games that Irish children enjoy. In pre-Christian times it was part of a great festival to honor the gods. At all the crossroads the

May Day is a time for spreading primroses on doorsteps and window sills.

people built huge bonfires to drive away evil spirits.

Later this festival became known as Bonfire Night. Boys and girls lit fires on top of hills to burn out the devils. As the fires blazed brightly in the darkness, the people danced and sang around them. When the dancing stopped, each took a blazing stick and made a charmed circle around crops, cattle, and houses. After the sacred fire died down, its coals were thrown on the crops to help bring a good harvest.

Most young people in today's Ireland think that Bonfire Night is for burning rubbish rather than devils. In some country areas, though, children say that their fathers and neighbors still throw coals from the dying fires on their cornfields.

Phillip McCarthy is a student in the highest grade of an elementary school in Ballyshannon, County Donegal. He describes how children in this area of Ireland celebrate Bonfire Night. "We had a big bonfire last night. Justin and his brother, Raymond, and my cousins and their friends came to it. We lit it about ten o'clock. And it was blazing up about half-time [half-past ten].

"We borrowed Jim Gavigan's saw and then got up the tree. We sawed down nearly half the tree. Then we went over to Jim Gavigan's and got eight tires. We threw the whole branches and tires on. Daddy helped us. Then we sat down around the bonfire. Mommy came out with biscuits and sweets. We ate away, and then when it got pitch dark we played around the fire. After that we had chips and beans. We ate away until we were fuller than before.

"We went back around the fire and played 'tip the can.' It's a game where you all hide, and if you're seen you have to try to 'tip the can.' We had to stop this because it was twelve o'clock, and Justin and Raymond had to go home. Then Rownie, my cousin, and I played 'keep the ball away' from Carl and Owen. At one o'clock we had to go to bed."

Later in the summer, on August 1, the Irish celebrate Lammas Day. In the past this was the feast day when special bread used at mass was made out of the newly-ripened corn. Today the Irish hold Lammas Fairs. The most famous is Puck Fair, which is held early in August.

Irish children enjoy going to the fair to see King Puck. On the first day this unusual king is dressed in ribbons, led into his cage, and hoisted high above the crowd. He does not seem to mind, though, for King Puck is a goat. After three days he is let down to earth again. The custom of honoring a goat began many years ago when goats warned the Irish of an enemy army advancing on a small town.

With the coming of the brisk days of fall, Irish children look forward to Halloween. In pre-Christian

King Puck is the center of attention at Puck Fair on Lammas Day.

times it was the eve of the Irish festival of Samhain, the Druid god of the dead. Druid priests built great bonfires on hilltops and burned animals and people alive to honor him. People believed that on that night spirits were everywhere because the dead returned to their homes. The flames from the fires were to guide friendly ghosts back home and frighten bad ones away.

When the Irish went outdoors on Samhain, they wore masks and costumes so that the evil spirits would not know who they were. These masked figures went around disguised as Muck Olla, a Druid god. Today Irish children celebrate Halloween by wearing masks and homemade costumes and "begging" from door to door.

Irish jack-o'-lanterns are quite different from American ones. Since pumpkins do not grow in Ireland, children carve funny faces on large turnips. When the Irish came to America many years ago, they discovered the many uses of pumpkins. In fact, Irish Americans started the tradition of carving jack-o'-lanterns.

Halloween actually started because the Irish celebrate All Saints' Day on November 1 in memory of their saints. Long ago it was called All Hallows' Day. The eve of All Hallows was known as All Hallows' Even. Later, it was shortened to Hallowe'en, and we call it Halloween.

With winter comes the Christmas season, a happy time for children in Ireland. On Christmas Eve a very old custom still takes place in many homes. The Christmas candle is placed in the window to welcome Mary and Joseph and Jesus. Then the youngest girl lights the candle. If there is no daughter in the family, the youngest boy lights it. The Irish have a saying: "The youngest child lives the longest and sends the custom fartherest."

On Christmas Eve the Christmas candle is placed in the window to welcome Mary and Joseph and Jesus.

On Christmas Eve or Christmas Day, Irish children attend mass with their parents. Afterward they open their presents, and the day ends with a special Christmas dinner for the whole family.

Saint Stephen's Day, the day after Christmas, is a holiday for everyone in Ireland. Long ago, according to Irish legend, Saint Stephen was hiding in a bush to escape from his enemies. A wren betrayed him. From that time on, the people hunted wrens on the day after Christmas. When a wren was killed, it was bound to a branch. Then, dressed in costumes, children went from house to house singing and asking for money. At the end of the day, they buried the wren.

Today the Irish observe this day in different ways in different parts of the country. In Galway children catch a wren at night and place it in a tin with airholes. Afterward they dress up in costumes and masks and go "mumming." Like the Christmas mummers of ancient Ireland, these modern day mummers perform plays of poetry verses. At the end of the day, the wren is set free.

"Wren boys" are a common sight in southern Ireland. In most parts of northern Ireland, though, children become mummers during the twelve days of Christmas. Instead of catching a wren, they go from home to home entertaining families during the Christmas season.

The holidays and festivals of the Irish year end with the Feast of the Holy Innocents, or Children's Day, on December 28. Families go to mass together, and the children take part in processions around the churches. All around the Irish year, young people and grown-ups have carried on the festive traditions that started long ago and have been passed down from generation to generation.

6. Of Irish Families

"If you are kind to your parents, you will have a long life," goes an old saying that is well known to Irish children. Boys and girls are taught to respect, honor, and obey their parents.

Grandparents are an important part of their home life, too. Once most grandparents lived in the same home as their grandchildren. In today's Ireland, though, many have their own small home closeby. "A hedge between, keeps the friendship green," is another Irish saying. Either way, grandparents are respected and are very much a part of Irish families.

Loyalty and respect are also shown among other family members. There are fewer divorces in Ireland than in most countries. Some say that Irish families stay together because the Catholic church does not allow divorces. Others believe that a special closeness exists between Irish husbands and wives.

Strong family ties are shown in different ways among Irish children. Brothers and sisters feel very responsible towards one another, and the older children share in the care of the younger ones. Even when the children grow up, it's not unusual for them to keep in close contact. Unmarried brothers and sisters sometimes live together. In one thatch-roofed cottage in Galway, a brother and sister in their eighties live in the home where both were born.

These strong family bonds make Irish children feel secure. Recently teenagers came from all over the Irish Republic to attend the annual Youth Science Conference. In a survey taken at the conference, most agreed that they came from happy families. Only a few said their families were unhappy.

Most of the teenagers had few complaints about family life. The eldest children liked being the oldest because they enjoyed the responsibility and freedom. Having special responsibilities wasn't always fun, though. "I must set a good example," said one teenager. "If my sister goes wrong, it is due to my bad influence," said another. Baby-sitting younger brothers and sisters instead of going out with friends was another complaint.

All of the teenagers in larger families noted certain things they did not like: having to put up with the rush to the "loo," or bathroom, in the morning; not having much money; not having their own room and privacy; and not being able to fit in the car with all the children. Even so, these young people liked being part of a large family.

Many of the teenagers live in "flats," city apartments of several rooms in a brick or concrete build-

An Irish grandfather enjoys a peaceful moment with his grandson.

ing. A large part of them live in neat houses or cottages with modern plumbing. These homes are made of the same materials and usually have four to six rooms.

Still other children, like Fiona Burke, live in farmhouses. Fiona lives in a 180-year-old Georgian farmhouse in the midlands. Young people living on farms have more chores than city children, for in the country every pair of hands is put to work.

In the small village of Knockvicar, the school day is over at ten past three. At home dinner is waiting. Afterward the children "wash up" and "dry up" the dishes. Homework comes next. Most Irish parents respect learning, and they expect their children to do well in school.

After homework, children do chores such as going to the shops for their "mums" or bringing in the cows for their fathers. During the turf-gathering seasons, boys and girls help bring in the turf.

Playtime is last. Both boys and girls play Gaelic football, a favorite Irish sport that combines parts of rugby and soccer. Cycling to a friend's house is something else children enjoy. If the hayloft is full, brothers and sisters climb up the ladder and have a great time running and jumping on the hay.

During Lent and other religious times, the young people of Knockvicar attend special evening prayers.

Some have already been to morning mass with their parents. Most young people sing in the church choir, which means that they go to choir practice on some evenings. Many attend band practice, too, because they belong to the youth band at Drumboylan. The band plays at festivals and in competitions. Practicing Irish songs and dances for the county *feis* contests is another evening activity.

In addition to this busy schedule, young people baby-sit, take messages to neighbors from their parents, and visit nearby friends and relatives. About eight o'clock they come home for tea. The children help again with the dishes. Then the family sits together and talks about daily events. Sometimes they watch television.

The Irish have one television network called RTE, which stands for *Radio Telefis Éireann*. The network is run by the government, and all owners of TV sets must pay yearly license fees to help support it.

On Friday evenings in Knockvicar, most families attend the Catholic church service. Afterward, they may take tea with nearby relatives. In Ireland, close ties between related families are common because their ancient Celtic heritage has helped to shape their way of life today.

"Saturday is our working day in our family," says nine-year-old Geraldine Smith. Making beds, doing dishes, bringing in the hay, and bringing home the turf are some of her Saturday chores.

Geraldine especially likes going to the creamery with her father because she gets to put the pipe into the creamery cans. The pipe carries the milk to a large tub where the milk is separated from the cream. The cream is made into butter and sold to nearby shops. Sometimes it is shipped to markets in Great Britain and Europe. When Geraldine's father is paid for the cream, the leftover skim milk is returned to him. He carries it home to feed the family's pigs.

Going down to the garden to pick a few heads of cabbage is Geraldine's next chore. She chops the cabbages and puts this favorite Irish vegetable in a saucepan with water. Weeding the cabbage patch and the rest of the vegetable garden is another of her Saturday jobs.

Before long it's time to set the table for dinner. After the meal, while her mother is busy washing the milking machine, Geraldine does the dishes. Later the family goes shopping in Boyle, a nearby town, and visits relatives there. Returning home, the children help prepare tea and bring in the cows. At the end of the day, everyone relaxes by watching TV until bedtime.

On Sundays most Irish children go to mass with their parents. In the Knockvicar area, a favorite place for mass is on Trinity Island in the middle of nearby Lough Key. This beautiful island park is similar to a state park in America. After mass and Sunday dinner, families may return to enjoy Lough Key. Here among the twenty-one islands in the lake, visitors come from all over the world to see the flower gardens and Irish deer.

For the schoolchildren of Knockvicar, summer holiday begins on July 1. Young people have lots of fun, but they must work hard, too, because summer is a busy time for Irish farmers. The first big job is to "save the hay." At haying time families work out in the fields for many hours at a time. Everyone is so busy that they even have tea outside. "It's great fun playing games like hide-and-go-seek around the hay after tea," says ten-year-old Mary McGovern. "Some years the weather is very bad and rainy for hay. Then we have to get it done quickly."

After all that work, it's time for some play. Young people may take a trip to Dublin with their parents. In the bustling capital, they visit the historic buildings and learn firsthand about their country's history. They also meet many new people and see the way of life in Ireland's largest city.

Children in Ireland's cities live much like city children in America. Some live in houses, while many others live in apartments called flats. Families have

The people of Knockvicar parish sometimes attend Sunday mass on Trinity Island in the middle of Lough Key.

Michéal Shivnan of Knockvicar parish "saves the hay" with the help of the McCormick children.

fewer children than in the country, and there are not as many chores for them to do. Still, boys and girls keep busy by joining youth and sports clubs, the Boy Scouts, and the Girl Guides (Girl Scouts).

Each community school has sports, singing, dancing, and recitation contests. In June Sports Day is held in schools all over Ireland. Students enter contests to win prizes for themselves and trophies for their schools. The winners go on to take part in the county finals.

Whether children live in the city or the country, the Catholic church plays an important part in their family life. The adults join its religious societies and take part in its social events. Irish children are taught to obey the rules of their church. Family members ask priests for advice about important decisions and personal problems. In many places, the local priest is the most important person in the community.

Eighteen-year-old Breeda Griffin attends school in the city of Limerick in southwest Ireland. Even though she lives away from home in a youth hostel, she is in close contact with the church. "The Catholic church rules our lives," says Breeda. "No matter what we're involved in, the church is always involved, too."

Older teenagers in Dublin and Cork have a bit more freedom than their country cousins in Knockvicar. They dress in the latest fashions, and they are more outspoken than country teenagers. Boys and girls go out together to movies, roller-discos, sports clubs, theaters, and the opera. Not too long ago, they did not mix freely either in school or social activities. Boys and girls had separate play yards and school entrances. Today they sit side by side in classrooms, and some high schools are even coeducational.

Teenagers date now, and a large number of them decide to get married. Once almost all young people in this age group remained single. Many lived with their parents until they were more than thirty years old. Since jobs and farmland were hard to find, they could not afford to get married. Now there are many jobs in the cities.

The roles of Irish men and women have changed, too. Once wives did not have the freedom to work outside the home. Now more than one-third of married women have paying jobs. One teacher said that although her husband is still the "breadwinner," she provides "the jam on the bread." The added income from working women also helps pay the mortgage on Ireland's neat, modern homes.

Whether or not the wife works, in recent years the role of the husband has changed. Many husbands now share in the care of the home and children. In the past many people would have been surprised to see an Irishman pushing a baby carriage.

In today's Ireland women meet in church social groups and clubs. Recently they have been going to a place that used to be reserved for men only—the neighborhood pub. For many years men have gone to the pub to drink beer and whiskey, play darts, and talk with friends. Now women enjoy going there, too. A growing number of pubs have sections for both men and women. Husbands and wives come for a glass of stout, a popular Irish black beer, and a "ploughman's lunch." This hearty meal is served at noon and includes bread and cheese.

Irish men and women do enjoy sharing good food, and they have much more to share today than during the Potato Famine of the 1840s. According to a United Nations report, Irish families are among the best fed in the world. Steak, lamb, bacon, ham, sausage, and chicken are everyday foods on Irish tables. Fresh vegetables, home-baked breads, rich milk and cream, butter, and cheese add variety to their meals.

Potatoes have been an important food for hundreds of years because they grow well in Ireland's wet, moist climate. The Irish have thought of many ways to use potatoes. Two of their favorites are potato pancakes and potato bread.

When the first Irish came to America, naturally they brought the potato with them. In 1719 Irish immigrants in Londonderry, New Hampshire, began

*The Shivnan family of Knockvicar parish at the table for high
tea:* (clockwise from the left) *Emer, Michael, Kathleen,
Mícheál, Áine, and Rhona.*

raising potatoes for food. Before long Americans
began to enjoy them, too. Today boiled new potatoes
remain one of the main vegetables on a New England
Fourth of July menu.

A favorite Irish meal using potatoes is Irish stew.
It is made by boiling layers of potatoes, onions, car-
rots, and pieces of lamb in a covered pot. Another
meal the Irish like is boiled salt pork, cabbage, and

potatoes. Caulcannon, a special dish, is made of mashed potatoes, parsnips, and onions.

Bread is also an important part of an Irish meal. Two very delicious homemade breads are brown wheaten loaf, and soda bread, which is often filled with currants, small, seedless raisins. Both of these tasty breads are made in flat round loaves.

Irish soda bread is not hard to make. For one loaf you will need:

4 cups whole wheat flour
2 cups plain flour
1-1/4 cups buttermilk (or sour milk)
1 teaspoon bicarbonate of soda
1 teaspoon salt
A large cutting board and baking sheet

Steps in the Recipe
1. Mix flour, soda, and salt and make a well.
2. Add milk to make a thick dough. Mix lightly and quickly. If dough is too stiff, add more milk (should not be wet).
3. With floured hands, put dough on a lightly-floured board. Flatten into a circle about 1-1/2 inches thick.
4. Place on baking sheet and make a large cross with floured knife.

5. Bake at 375° for 40 minutes. Test center with a skewer (will not stick when done.)
6. To keep bread soft, wrap in a clean tea towel.

The Irish always seem to be eating a meal or drinking tea. They begin with a hearty breakfast, which may include cereal, bacon, eggs, sausages, fried tomato halves, homebaked bread, and tea. American-style cornflakes is their favorite cereal. Dinner, which is eaten in the middle of the day, is another hearty meal. At this time the Irish usually have soup, meat, potatoes, and other vegetables.

Low tea is served early in the afternoon. Sometimes special treats accompany the tea—little muffins called scones with butter and jam, cakes, and cookies. For high tea, which is served as a supper early in the evening, cold meats, fish, salads, freshly-baked bread, and more cakes and biscuits may be on the table. Finally, at nine or ten in the evening, the Irish eat a light snack before bed. Another steaming pot of tea is served then, for Irish evenings are chilly even in summer.

Customs, climate, and history make Irish families different from those in North America. The people do not have as many cars and television sets and other things that we often take for granted. Still, most Irish families are strong, close, loving, and happy.

7. *From Hedges to Classrooms*

The sky for a roof! Hedges for walls! And stones for seats! In the 1700s, when the English banned all Catholic schools, many Irish children had to go to a school in the great outdoors.

Children who attended these secret Hedge Schools in the fields were in constant danger. Anyone who had reached the age of sixteen could be arrested and sent to court. One student was placed on guard to watch for strangers coming along the mud road. They could be informers, or people who received a reward for telling the English soldiers where a Hedge school was. Once the guard spied a stranger, everyone would scatter like leaves before the wind!

If an Irish schoolmaster was caught, he was sent into slavery in the West Indies or shipped to the American colonies. Many became the first teachers of the children of the American colonists.

These talented schoolmasters were excellent teachers. Some were descended from scholars and poets in the days of the Irish high kings. Setting up schools wherever they went, they traveled from one colony to another. In some places a farmer would help by providing a barn.

In Ireland anyone who provided shelter for a Catholic school would be treated harshly. To avoid danger, all classes had to be held outdoors. In winter a sod house was scooped out of the bank on the roadside, and smoke from a small fire escaped through a hole in the mud roof. Even the poorest child brought two sods of turf to keep the fire going.

Schoolmasters in those days received strange pay. Some parents were too poor to pay anything. Most, however, gave up something they needed themselves—a basket of potatoes, a dozen eggs, a chicken, or milk. At Easter and Christmas, a fresh roll of butter was a welcome gift. A few children did pay in money. Still, the schoolmaster's salary for the whole year was sometimes only eighty dollars!

Since there were no textbooks in Hedge Schools, the schoolmaster taught each subject from memory. Students learned to read by studying adult books. Writing, arithmetic, catechism, or questions and answers about the beliefs of the Catholic religion, geography, Greek, and Latin were the other subjects.

Today Irish students no longer sit on stones in open fields. In rural areas the schools are usually one-story concrete buildings. Even in the cities, though, Irish schools are not as large and modern as schools in North America.

Most schools in the Irish Republic are run by the

Roman Catholic church and the Church of Ireland, a Protestant church. The government provides most of the funds to support the schools. Children from the ages of six to fifteen are required to go to school, and most education through high school is free.

Since the Catholic church runs a large number of schools, many Irish children learn their catechism every day. The local priest rules over all of their education. He chooses the principal, and he approves the hiring of each teacher. Schools in the United States are run differently because the U.S. Constitution provides that church and government powers must be separate.

To understand how Irish schools work, let's pretend that we are visiting the school at Knockvicar. In one classroom boys and girls are high stepping through a lively folk dance. In another room, a child is reciting a poem in Gaelic which was written by Padraic Pearse about the 1916 Easter Rebellion. In the room combining the fifth, sixth, and seventh "standards," or grades, boys and girls are singing in Gaelic about the great Potato Famine of the 1840s. In the song, an Irishman asks a friend abroad to come back to the land of his birth.

All of these children are practicing for the local yearly feis contests. If they win the grand prize, they will go on to the county finals.

Irish schoolchildren in the classroom and outside during recess at a school in County Roscommon. On the wall in the rear of the classroom is a picture of Pope John Paul II.

Dancing, poetry, and singing are school activities that many Irish young people enjoy. During the school day, though, students spend most of their time studying more serious subjects.

A typical school day starts at half-past nine because in many parts of Ireland, children have early morning farm chores to do. Two brothers, ten and eleven, have seven cows to milk and eight chickens, a mother cat, and her kittens to feed. Others have to "tidy up" the kitchen and their bedrooms and "wash up" the dishes. All these chores must be done before school starts.

One Irish boy reports that "the master collects me at quarter past nine." The Irish master, or principal, picks up this boy because he lives in a mountainous area where the small school bus does not go.

Since the Catholic church runs most schools, the school day starts with a prayer. Students at Knockvicar work at sums, or math, until eleven o'clock. After a fifteen-minute recess, they have lessons in English and Gaelic. History and geography are studied next. A favorite part of the world for Irish students is North America. They learn about the Great Lakes, the Mississippi River, and the Golden Gate Bridge in San Francisco. Many Irish children think about coming to North America to see what it is like.

At noon boys and girls study catechism. Then

they go outside, eat lunch, and play until it's time to study history and geography again. On some days the children have nature study or singing and drawing. Each Monday they take an hour of physical education. The school day usually ends at ten-past three.

Back home again from school in Knockvicar, young people eat dinner, help clean up the kitchen, and do their homework. Then the cows must be brought to the barn and milked again. Children are kept busy learning and helping.

Sean Bambrick of Knockvicar parish milks his family's cows early each morning before he goes to school.

Parents of today's Catholic students were kept even busier than their children. Until recent years students were expected to help keep the schools warm and clean. Their families were required to bring one or two donkey cart loads of turf to keep the stove going.

Students brought soap and towels for washing up and for cleaning the schoolroom. Each day they were assigned to do special jobs such as sweeping, dusting, and washing windows. The teacher followed orders from the parish priest, and he received his instructions from the Department of Education. The priest had to raise the money to pay all the costs of the schools in his parish.

During the 1970s the Department of Education made some changes in the way the schools are run. School boards of management were set up throughout Ireland so that parents could become more involved in the education of their children. Two parent representatives and one teacher serve on each school board. The parish priest heads the board, and the bishop is also a member along with the people he appoints to serve with him. On all boards the church members outnumber the parents and teachers.

From the very beginning, the teachers did not think that the new Catholic school system was fair. As it stands now, the teachers and the parents together are never able to outvote the others on the board. They believe that they should have just as many votes as the church members have.

The church, however, will not agree to their wishes because it wants to keep control over the education of Catholic children. Both sides think that they are right. Since the church refuses to make any changes, the teachers will not serve on the boards. On the other hand, in some areas bishops will not allow the boards to operate at all.

The school management boards do work well in many ways. They take care of heating, cleaning, and repairing buildings. If money is needed for equipment and other things, the board makes a special request to the government.

Sometimes a new school is needed. Ten years ago the parish of the Knockvicar area asked for a new building. The Department of Education agreed to provide almost all of the money for it, and construction began at that time. Two years later the funds ran out. Years later the rest of the money was provided.

Saint Michael's and Saint Patrick's National School, Cootehall, is now complete. The students from four very old and small schools in the parish were assigned to the new one. Only three of the schools have sent their pupils to the new building. The other school refuses to send its students there

Saint Michael's and Saint Patrick's National School, Coote-hall, the new school in Knockvicar parish. Standing together by the school (left, rear) *are Michéal Shivnan, the school principal, and Father H. Harte, the school manager.*

because it wants to keep its own Gaelic football team and dramatic, singing, and dancing groups. This school also believes that the new school is too far away for young children to walk to and that its classes are too large for students to learn well.

Like the new primary school at Knockvicar, most

secondary schools are run by the Catholic church. The Irish government provides most of the money for these schools, too. Students are from twelve to nineteen years old, and they must stay in school until they are fifteen. In recent years no fees have been charged at almost all of the day secondary schools. The government hopes that free education will encourage young men and women to stay in Ireland and continue their schooling.

Some secondary schools are called trade schools. They teach subjects that help young people learn a trade in courses of study that last from one to three years. At the end of the courses, students who pass an exam earn a certificate. This is now required to enter many skilled trades.

In some areas "comprehensive" and "community" schools have been set up at the secondary level. These schools offer both regular courses and trade skill courses under one roof.

The highest level of education in the Irish Republic is the two universities. The National University of Ireland, a Catholic school, has three branches in Dublin, Cork, and Galway. The University of Dublin, also called Trinity College, is a Protestant school. Catholics must ask their bishop for permission to study there. Trinity College is known around the world for its excellent programs.

These two older universities are no longer able to meet the demand by the Irish for advanced education. To provide more opportunities for young people, ten regional colleges have been established. Students are able to take many technical courses at these schools. Recently, a new one opened in Tralee.

In the future more of these colleges will be opened. Irish students have come a long way since they studied in fields in the secret Hedge Schools. No longer do they have to flee from threatening English soldiers. Now their great pride in learning is out in the open for everyone to see.

8. *Hurley Sticks and Horses*

Like baseball in America, hurling is an Irish sport that has stood the test of time. The Irish invented the game more than four thousand years ago, and many of their early heroes were champion hurlers. A legend called The Red Branch tells of Cuchulainn's great skill with his *caman*, or hurley stick. He killed the king's fierce guard dog with a ball delivered off his hurley. Fairies played the game in many of the old fairy tales.

Hurling is often called the fastest field game in the world, and it is one of the most exciting, too. All the players use hurleys to hit a small leather ball. Hurleys are like very broad, flat hockey sticks, about four feet long and curved at the bottom. Since ancient days, they have been carved from the ash tree.

The broad base of the hurley keeps the tennis-size ball moving at great speed. Sometimes the ball travels so fast that people watching the game lose sight of it. Because of the hard ball and the fast-moving camans, hurling can be dangerous.

Like field hockey, the object of hurling is to drive the ball into the opposing team's goal. Three points are scored when the ball goes under the crossbar of the goal. If the ball goes over it, one point is made. To move the ball about the field, players must be skilled and have strong wrists for changing the direction of play.

The Gaelic Athletic Association plans hurling games in all of Ireland's parishes, counties, and provinces. At the final, which is held each year in September in Croke Park in Dublin, 75,000 people jam the stadium. For the Irish this game is just as exciting as the World Series, Super Bowl, or Stanley Cup is to us. Every schoolboy dreams of playing in the All-Ireland Hurling Final!

Irish young people also dream of playing in the All-Ireland Football Final. Gaelic football is another favorite national sport. Like hurling, the final is held in Croke Park in September.

This sport has not been played in Ireland for as long as hurling. Centuries ago, when the Normans ruled Galway, the Irish were using hurleys as weapons against them. Upset by the hurley stick attacks, the Normans ordered the people to play the game "with the great ball" instead of the ancient sport of hurling. The ball was made of ox-hide and "stuffed with finest hay." Forced to play this new game, the Irish did not take long to develop their own style—Gaelic football.

While in some ways Gaelic football is like American football, in other ways it is like soccer. The ball

Young athletes charge after the ball during a Gaelic football match in Dublin's Croke Park.

used by the Irish is round. Body charging is allowed but tackling is not. As in hurling, a ball that goes over the crossbar counts one point. A ball that goes under the bar is a goal and earns three points.

There are more than 3,000 Gaelic football clubs in Ireland, 160 in Great Britain, 30 in North America, and a few in Australia. Play-offs for the All-Ireland Final begin in Irish counties each April. Sports fans who are not able to go to the games watch them on television or listen to them on radio.

Irish boys and girls are great fans of Gaelic football and hurling, and many of them take part in these sports. Young people in the cities spend much time on the playing fields of the parks. Often a group of boys will be playing a hurling match or a football game. If no park is nearby, the young athletes practice football in the street.

Irish boys and girls from age eight to seventeen take part in parish community games. These games cover everything from Gaelic football to chess, and more than a half-million young people in all of Ireland's thirty-two counties take part. Each community includes parishes within a ten-mile area. In Knockvicar Sports Day is held early in June. Later the winners of this local event compete in the county finals.

In September the winners from the county finals gather at Butlin's Holiday Camp in Mosney, County Meath, for the national contests. For two weekends the camp becomes a little Olympic-style village. There are parades, opening ceremonies, lighting of the games torch, and gold, silver, and bronze medals for the top finishers. Both the youngsters and the adults who come to watch them have lots of fun.

When the Irish aren't busy with the parish community games, they may be playing a very unusual game. In some parts of Ireland, the Irish bowl on the open road. Road bowling is an exciting game that is played with an iron ball called a "bullet."

In this contest, two players throw the bullet to a distant finish line from two to three miles away. The one who takes the fewest throws wins. In road bowling players must throw the ball around curves and over bridges and brooks. People watching them make bets on the players. They also have to step lively when the bullet rolls their way!

Coursing, the sport of dog racing, has been popular in Ireland for hundreds of years. Greyhounds, a swift, long legged breed, are the racers. At first they hunted hares. Now they chase the hares on a racing track to see which greyhound can catch a hare first. Fortunately, the hares have been trained to escape by dashing through small openings that are too narrow for the dogs to follow.

People place bets on the greyhounds just as they bet on racing horses. The winning dogs become as famous as Ireland's leading hurling and football players. One greyhound, Mick the Miller, won nineteen big races in a row. Later he became a movie star. When he died, Mick was stuffed and placed on view in the London Natural History Museum.

Since Ireland is famous for its fine horses, it's not surprising that the people like horse racing even more than dog racing. In fact, horse racing is called the

Greyhound racing (top) *and horse racing* (bottom) *are two popular Irish sports.*

sport of kings. The Irish have enjoyed it for more than two thousand years.

Two horse races are known around the world: the Irish Derby, which is held each year at Kildare in June; and the Irish Grand National, which is held near Dublin during Easter week. Horses from many countries are entered in both of these events. Ireland presents some of the largest cash prizes in world racing.

As early as 1752, the Irish invented a special kind of horse racing called steeplechasing. A steeplechase is a cross-country race in which horse and rider jump over hedges, ditches, banks, and stone walls. It was first run in County Cork. The race began at Buttevant, and the riders were told to race as far as the Doneraile Church steeple. That is how the sport got its name.

More than two thousand of Ireland's finest horses are entered in the Royal Dublin Society Horse Show each August. Many horses and riders come from foreign countries to take part in this grand jumping show. Young people compete in events of their own: junior races, jumping contests, and dressage, or guiding a horse through a set of exercises without using reins, hands or legs.

The week of the horse show is an exciting one for the thousands of people who travel to Dublin to see the events. Bagpipe bands with kilted pipers lead national jumping teams past the flower-bordered

A horse leaps over a barrier during a contest at the Dublin Horse Show.

stands. Riders dress in brightly colored riding habits. Their boots are highly polished. All of them, from the oldest to the youngest rider, hope to win a prize!

Horses are used in two other Irish sports, pony-

Young people pony-trekking in County Mayo.

trekking and caravanning. In pony-trekking, a small group of riders meets at a stable and climbs up into the hills and mountains. After a few hours, they reach the goal of their trek, which is often a small cottage.

There lunch is served to the hungry travelers. After the ponies have been fed, watered, and rested, the riders mount again and make the trek back down to the stables.

Caravanning is not for anyone in a hurry. A caravan is a horse-drawn house on wheels which has bunk beds and a stove. It is the same kind of wagon that the tinkers once used. Caravans rumble along the

The back roads of County Mayo are being explored by these young caravanners.

back roads, covering about eight or nine miles a day. Ireland is a good place for caravanning because many of its roads are free from heavy traffic. Along the way caravanners often stop for a friendly chat with the local farmers and townspeople.

The Irish who aren't pony-trekking or caravanning may be fishing, for Ireland is one of the best places to fish in the world. Its lakes, rivers, streams, and coastal waters are filled with many kinds of fish — salmon, brown trout, pike, and others. A favorite place to fish is the Shannon River. This long, winding waterway is also a popular place for sailing and waterskiing.

Many Irish teenagers spend their free time exploring the countryside. They cycle, hike, and mountain climb. More than fifty years ago, the Irish formed *An Óige,* the youth hostel group, because they wanted their young people to enjoy the outdoors. To make it easy for them to keep the cost down, An Óige opened overnight sleeping places, or hostels, all over the country.

At Foulksrath in County Kilkenny, backpackers stay in a sixteenth-century castle. The Irish people donated money to purchase and restore it as a hostel. The castle is open to all An Óige members, and visitors are always welcome from fifty other youth hostel groups around the world.

In addition to the youth hostels, the Irish have set aside many areas for park lands. Most parks have nature trails and camping and picnic sites. Irish families can camp or caravan or stay in small hotels nearby.

Muckross National Park in Killarney, County Kerry, is the most beautiful park of all. Here in a broad valley are three lakes framed by purple-misted mountains — the highest in Ireland. The lakes are filled with small wooded islands. Thick green grass and flowering trees and plants make Muckross a place of beauty. The grounds are thick with rhododendrons, and hawthorns, fuchsias, wild roses, honeysuckle, silver birches, ferns, and ivy grow here, too.

Perched on the edge of Lough Leane is Muckross Manor, a great grey stone house built three hundred years ago. Inside, the manor is filled with books, crafts, and furnishings from the Irish past. Nearby are the ruins of Muckross Abbey, built by monks in the 1400s. In this ancient, sacred building are the tombs of the poets of Kerry.

No cars or buses are allowed on the park's narrow roads. Visitors may travel on foot, by bicycle, or by jaunting car, a little four-seated horsecart. The drivers are called *jarveys*. As the horse clip-clops along the path, they may tell an Irish story or talk about the history of the park.

One of the beautiful lakes of Killarney in Muckross National Park.

Muckross National Park was given to the people of Ireland by an American, Arthur Vincent. Once he and his wife Maud lived there. In 1929 Maud Vincent died. Mr. Vincent decided to give his historic estate to the Irish people in memory of his wife.

When Arthur Vincent turned his land over to the Irish Free State in 1932, he expressed his vision of its future. "I want especially to have the young people come to Muckross, to trail these mountains, and to enjoy nature in all its aspects. I hope that Muckross will be a real garden of friendship, and that it will be the greatest playground in the world."

Since that day the park has grown more lovely than ever. Irish young people still enjoy this beautiful playground, and it remains a true "garden of friendship" between America and Ireland.

9. No Irish
Need Apply

The Irish have always been travelers. One Irish story tells about a man from Cork, whose dream was to reach the end of the world.

He traveled many a weary mile. At last he came to a great wall that reached nearly to the sky. Up he went from rock to rock. At the very top he found a man from Kerry, calmly smoking his pipe and gazing off into space.

The people of Galway say that Columbus stopped off there on his way to the New World. They might add that an Irishman, by the name of Rice de Culvey, shipped on board to see that he got there.

Written records show that the Irish arrived in North America in the 1600s. Catholic families fleeing from harsh English rule settled in Pennsylvania and Maryland. The Protestant Scotch-Irish from Ulster arrived before the American Revolution.

Many of these Irish fought in the Revolutionary Army. Such names as Murphy, Sullivan, Kelly, Burke, and Donovan were in the famous "Line of Ireland" unit. Before one battle, General George Washington ordered that the signal, or watchword, be "Saint Patrick."

John Barry, born in Wexford County, Ireland, was the captain of the first American fighting ship. In 1777 he captured five British ships during one battle. General Washington sent him a message congratulating him for his great victory. Later he was called the "Father of the American Navy."

When the war was over, Irishmen helped form the government of the new United States of America. Four signers of the Declaration of Independence were of Irish birth. Another five were of Irish descent.

One of the most well known was Charles Thomson from County Derry. This Irish immigrant wrote the final draft of the Declaration of Independence. From 1774 to 1789, he served as secretary of the Continental Congress. This group declared America's independence from England and formed the United States of America. Thomson helped run the elections for the first U.S. Congress and president. He also designed the Great Seal of the United States.

James Hoban, an Irish architect from County Kilkenny, designed the White House in the new United States capital, Washington, D.C. His prize-winning 1792 design was inspired by three important buildings in Ireland. One was Leinster House, which is now the meeting place of the Irish Parliament. Recently the U.S. government issued a stamp that shows Hoban alongside the White House.

Most of Ireland's sons and daughters did not have the skills of Thomson and Hoban. Many of those arriving between 1815 and 1860 were tenant farmers from southern Ireland. They had been pushed off their lands by greedy landlords and could no longer make a living.

During the great Potato Famine, the few farmers with land were no better off than the landless peasants. Hundreds of thousands died from hunger and disease. The English did little to help the Irish. Finally many Irish had to choose between dying and leaving their country. A million and a half people decided to leave, and most chose to go to America.

Families packed their few belongings. To begin the long journey, some had to walk many miles to seaports. They slept in fields and ate cabbage leaves and weeds.

On the ships conditions were no better than in Ireland. The poor slept in steerage, the deck below the waterline. There was little fresh air, and the cooking odors and the lack of toilets made a terrible smell. No water was allowed for bathing. The bunks for sleeping were stacked on top of each other. They were four feet wide, and four slept in a bunk! If the wind died down, the trip lasted eight to ten weeks. No wonder people became ill and died on these "coffin" ships.

One can imagine how happy the Irish were to set

foot on America's shores. Some had brought little bags of Ireland's soil. When they landed, they mixed it with the earth of their new home.

The ill went to the hospital. Those who were still well were greeted by "runners." These crafty agents said they were there to help the newly arrived immigrants. They wore green bow ties to make the weary travelers think they were Irish. Some even used fake Irish brogues, or accents.

These runners were really there to cheat and trick the Irish. They took them to lodging houses where the rates were very high. Before long the poor immigrants had used up all their money. Because they owed their landlords, they could not leave to find a cheaper place.

Sometimes the agents offered to sell them railroad tickets. Later the Irish learned that the tickets would take them only part of the way. Then they were told that only a short walk remained at the end of their train ride. In fact, the "short walk" was often hundreds of miles.

In 1853 a place called Castle Gardens was opened to protect the immigrants from the runners. There the Irish could buy railroad tickets, change their money into American dollars, and find out about jobs. Castle Gardens helped many new arrivals before it closed in 1892 when the U.S. government opened Ellis Island.

In the beginning, however, everything seemed to go wrong for the Irish. With little or no money, most had to settle in the large seaport cities of the East Coast—New York, Boston, and Philadelphia. Though they were country people, the Irish were now forced to be city people.

Those who were lucky found jobs as laborers, servants, and carters, the drivers of delivery wagons. Many became policemen. In 1855 most of the police officers in New York City were born in Ireland.

The unlucky ones begged for food and slept in cellars of old, rundown buildings. Their new life was not much different from the terrible life they had left behind. And now they could not see the lovely green fields and hills of home.

The Irish were paid very low wages—$.50 to $1.50 a day. An Irish serving woman working for a rich family earned four to seven dollars a month plus room and board.

Since they could not afford decent housing, many families had to share a windowless basement room. Often they had to put up with rats and knee-deep water. Most of the Irish stayed together in areas of the cities called "Little Irelands." In New York many settled on the Lower East Side, a poor area where rents were low.

Those who could not afford to rent went north of

the city. Since they built small shacks, or "shanties," Americans called them the "Shanty Irish." Some of the new immigrants were known as the "Lace Curtain Irish." They could afford to hang white lace curtains at their windows.

Most Americans disliked all the Irish. They believed the newcomers were bringing poverty, crime, and disease to America and would lower workers' wages because they were willing to work for less. Most of all, they feared these "foreigners" because they were Catholic.

By 1850 more than a million and a half Catholics had already come to the United States. The Protestants felt they would become too strong. Rumors spread that the Catholics planned to bring the pope to America and turn the country over to him. Soon signs began to appear on the front of shops and factories saying, "Man wanted. No Irish need apply."

In turn, the Catholics disliked the Protestants. Every day in the public schools, Catholic children had to listen to a reading from the Protestant Bible. Many Catholics decided to keep their children at home. They wanted their children to learn, but they also wanted them to "keep the faith." This saying was often used by the Irish in place of "good bye."

To provide education for its young people, the Catholic church began building its own schools. Parents of students were asked to pay a small amount of money to help support Catholic education. Even the poorest parents agreed. Before long, many Irish became doctors, lawyers, and judges. They gave the church money to build Catholic colleges and universities. Today there are many of these schools all over the country.

Though most Irish stayed in the large eastern cities, thousands found work out in the American frontier lands. The people living in these areas had very few supplies. By helping to build roads, canals, and railroads, the Irish laborers were able to get these goods through to them.

The Irish workers were called "paddies" because so many of them were named Patrick. The paddies were strong and willing to work long hours clearing land and laying tracks. They helped build the eastern railroads and the Union Pacific line, the first coast-to-coast American railroad.

Like the runners, the railroad foremen cheated the Irish. On payday they sometimes disappeared with the payroll.

The paddies in the coal mines of Pennsylvania and West Virginia fared no better than the railroad workers. A miner was paid for each carload of coal that he dug. During the night, the mine operator often switched the smaller car the miner had agreed to

Irish workers helped build America's railroads. In this 1868 photo, railway workers clear the right of way for the Union Pacific line, the first U.S. coast-to-coast railroad.

fill for a larger one. The paddy would have to fill it because he needed money for his family and his church. He would also send some of his hard-earned pay to relatives and friends in Ireland.

Many Irish workers in the cities worked long hours for low wages in the clothing factories. They were paid by the "piece," or finished article. After working all day in these "sweat shops," they usually earned no more than a dollar!

After years of being cheated, the paddies began to fight back. Sometimes they would riot and tear up railroad tracks. At other times a cruel foreman would be found dead.

Many Irish believed that workers could find peaceful ways to improve working conditions. In 1851 the Convention of Irish Societies was formed. This group asked workers in each company to join together and to elect leaders to discuss unfair rules with the company owners. It also asked everyone to pay dues to help the sick and those out of work.

The Convention of Irish Societies was the beginning of today's labor unions. Many Irish are still the leaders in these unions. During the past century, labor groups have improved the working conditions and wages of millions of workers.

Another early Irish group in New York City was called the Society of Saint Tammany. It began to help immigrants in 1846, and later it became known as Tammany Hall. The city was divided into districts with an elected leader in each district. Each district leader provided food, jobs, and housing for the poor and hungry. Many Irishmen entered politics through Tammany Hall.

Catholics began to help Catholic candidates in city and state elections. In 1918 Alfred E. Smith became governor of New York. Ten years later, when he ran for president, he lost. Many Americans still believed that a Catholic president would be loyal to the pope instead of the United States.

John Fitzgerald Kennedy, a young U.S. senator from Massachusetts, was a fine speaker with Irish charm and wit. In 1960 he won a close election to become the first Catholic president of the United States. The Irish rejoiced everywhere, but those in County Wexford were the most happy of all!

The Kennedys had left County Wexford in 1850 to escape the Potato Famine. Patrick Kennedy, who was born in Boston, worked as a saloon-keeper. His grandson, Joseph Kennedy, became a bank president and the first Irishman to serve as U.S. ambassador to England. Joseph's dream was that someday one of his sons would become president of the United States.

John F. Kennedy, Joseph's son, was a beloved president who was loyal only to his country. People

John F. Kennedy was the first Catholic president of the United States.

around the world were saddened when he was shot to death in November 1963. This Irish American will always be remembered for the challenge he gave in his inaugural address: "Ask not what your country can do for you, but what you can do for your country."

In November 1980, another Irish American was elected to the U.S. presidency. His name is Ronald Reagan.

People of Irish descent have proved themselves in other fields besides politics. There have been many talented Irish-American playwrights and novelists. Eugene O'Neill, John O'Hara, and F. Scott Fitzgerald are among the most famous.

Eugene O'Neill's father came to America as a child after the Potato Famine. His son became America's greatest playwright. O'Neill was the second American to win the Nobel Prize for literature, and he won the Pulitzer Prize for drama four times.

Other Irish Americans wrote fine songs that we enjoy playing and singing today. Edward MacDowell, Victor Herbert, and George M. Cohan are the best known of these songwriters. One of Cohan's songs is "I'm a Yankee Doodle Dandy." Born in Dublin, Victor Herbert wrote many light operas. Young people enjoy his *Babes in Toyland.*

Irish Americans James Cagney, Helen Hayes, Pat O'Brien, Gene Kelly, and Bing Crosby have acted in a great many movies and plays. Another big star of Irish descent, Marion Michael Morrison, is better known to his fans as John Wayne. In television, Carroll O'Connor, star of "All in the Family," has entertained millions as Archie Bunker.

The Irish have made their mark in sports, too. In 1877 John L. Sullivan decided to become a boxer. One night he stepped out of the crowd into the boxing ring. Winning that match, he went on to become the heavyweight champion of the world. Sullivan helped introduce new boxing rules, and he became a hero to the American people. In 1892 he was defeated by another fine Irish boxer, "Gentleman Jim" Corbett. Jack Dempsey, Jim Braddock, and Gene Tunny were other boxing champions of Irish descent.

The football world has honored such Irish players as Jim Crowley and Elmer Layden of Notre Dame. Connie Mack was a famous baseball player and manager who was elected to baseball's Hall of Fame.

Without the contributions of Irish Americans, American cities would not have grown as fast as they did. Louis Henry Sullivan was America's first modern architect. The son of a wandering Irish musician, he designed the first modern American skyscraper.

New York City became one of the East Coast's finest harbors thanks to another Irishman. John Wolfe Ambrose directed the dredging of a deep-water channel so that huge ships could enter the port. A beacon that guides the ships into the harbor is called Ambrose Light.

John MacDonald, the son of Irish immigrants

Henry Ford at his desk with a model of the Model T behind him (upper left).

from Tipperary, was in charge of building the New York City subway system. When he died in 1911, all power was shut down for two minutes in his honor.

Emmet J. McCormack became the head of one of the largest steamship lines in the world. McCormack started out as a young boy selling coal and rope near the New York City waterfront. To get his first ship, he offered to raise a sunken ferryboat if he could use it for six years. The boat was raised from the deep, and before long it was joined by many more.

The inventor who put millions of North Americans on wheels was the son of a man from County Cork. Henry Ford developed the Model T and started his own company to make it on an assembly line. Today the Ford Motor Company is one of the world's largest car manufacturers.

Many others of Irish descent, both famous and unknown, have helped to make life better in North America. They have come a long way since the signs, "No Irish need apply," hung in shop windows. Once laughed at because of their clothes, brogue, customs, and religion, the Irish today have earned the respect of the people of their adopted country. They are proud to call themselves Americans.

But wherever the Irish go, one thing 'tis sure— they will never turn their backs on the special ways that make them Irish!

Appendix

Irish Consulates in the United States and Canada

The Irish consulates in the United States and Canada want to help Americans and Canadians understand Irish ways. For information and resource materials about Ireland, contact the consulate or embassy nearest you.

U.S. Consulates

Boston, Massachusetts
　　Consulate General of Ireland
　　535 Boylston Street
　　Boston, Massachusetts 02116
　　Phone (617) 267-9330
Chicago, Illinois
　　Consulate General of Ireland
　　400 N. Michigan Avenue
　　Chicago, Illinois 60611
　　Phone (312) 337-1868
San Francisco, California
　　Consulate General of Ireland
　　681 Market Street
　　San Francisco, California 94105
　　Phone (415) 392-4214
Washington, D.C.
　　Consular Office and Embassy of Ireland
　　2234 Massachusetts Avenue NW
　　Washington, D.C. 20008
　　Phone (202) 483-7639

Canadian Embassy

　　Embassy of Ireland
　　170 Metcalfe Street
　　Ottawa, Ontario K2P 1P3
　　Phone (613) 233-6281

Glossary

árd-rí—the Irish high king who ruled over lesser kings centuries ago

banshee—a lone fairy woman with a high, wailing voice who foretold death in the ruling families of ancient Ireland

bawneen—a special undyed wool used for knitting clothes in the Aran Islands

bean feasa—an old woman with magical powers

caman—a stick used to hit a small leather ball in the game of hurling

céad mile fáilte—"a hundred thousand welcomes"

cluideog—about a dozen eggs

crannog—an island built by ancient Irish kings for their family and cattle

currach—a skin- or canvas-covered boat used in the past by the fishermen of the Aran Islands; some currachs are still in use today

Éire—the Gaelic name for Ireland

far darrig—a mischievous fairy called the "red man"

feis—a contest among schoolchildren to test their abilities and talents in singing, dancing, and recitation

filid—an ancient Irish poet who recited laws and legends from memory

Gaeltacht—an area in Ireland where the Irish still speak Gaelic and follow the old customs

jarvey—a driver of a jaunting car

Lia Fa'l—the "Stone of Destiny" upon which the árd-rí placed his hand while being sworn in as the high king of Ireland

lough—a lake

Mac—the son of; it was added to many Irish names during the reign of Brian Boru

O—the grandson of; also added to many Irish names during the reign of Brian Boru

púca—a lone fairy of the spirit world; the púca can appear in the form of a frightening black horse

rath—a fairy fort made by a small mound of dirt enclosed by a ring of trees or rocks

rí—the king who headed each Celtic family and ruled over a territory known as a tuath

seanchais—wandering storytellers of ancient Ireland

sleann—a spade used to cut turf into blocks

tuath—the territory ruled by the rí who headed each Celtic family

Selected Bibliography

Alderman, Clifford. *The Wearing of the Green.* New York: Julian Messner, 1972.

Barth, Edna. *Witches, Pumpkins, and Grinning Ghosts.* New York: Seabury Press, 1972.

Bulla, Clyde. *New Boy in Town.* New York: Thomas Y. Crowell Co., 1969.

Colum, Padraic. *The Treasury of Irish Folklore.* New York: Crown Publishers, 1962.

Dobrin, Arnold. *Ireland, The Edge of Europe.* Nashville: Thomas Nelson, 1970.

Eadue, Peter; Duff, Cyril; and Caldwell, John. *Let's Visit Ireland.* New York: John Day, 1968.

Erdoes, Richard. *Bewitching Wonderland.* New York: Dodd, Mead, & Co., 1968.

Fagen, Rhoda et al. *Ireland in Pictures.* New York: Sterling Publishing Co., 1978.

Haining, Peter. *The Leprechaun's Kingdom.* New York: Harmony Books, 1980.

Jacobs, Joseph. *More Celtic Fairy Tales.* New York: G.P. Putnam's Sons, 1902.

Johnson, James. *The Irish in America.* Minneapolis: Lerner Publications, 1976.

MacManus, Seumas. *Hibernian Nights.* New York: MacMillan, 1963.

McCarthy, Joe. *Ireland.* New York: Time Life Books, 1964.

McDonnell, Virginia. *The Irish Helped Build America.* New York: Julian Messner, 1969.

Murray, Bridget. *Calendar of Irish Folk Customs, 1981.* Belfast, Northern Ireland: Appleton Press (distributed by Irish Books and Media, Saint Paul, Minnesota).

O'Brien Educational. *Families and Friends: Irish Town Life in Story, Poem, and Picture.* Dublin, Ireland: O'Brien International, 1978 (distributed by Irish Books and Media, Saint Paul, Minnesota).

O'Faolain, Eileen. *Irish Sagas and Folk Tales.* London: Oxford University Press, 1964.

Quigley, Lillian Fox. *Ireland.* New York: MacMillan, 1964.

Sheehy, Terence. *Ireland in Color.* New York: W.W. Norton & Co., 1975.

Uris, Jill, and Uris, Leon. *Ireland, A Terrible Beauty.* New York: Doubleday Publishing Co., 1975.

Yeats, W.B. *Irish Fairy and Folk Tales.* New York: Boni & Liveright, 1918.

Index

142

About the Author

As the preschool director and creative writing teacher at Saint Matthew's Episcopal Day School in San Mateo, California, Kathleen Allan Meyer works with young people to improve their ability to express themselves through writing.

A visit to Ireland in 1977 reawakened the author's interest in her Irish ancestry. To prepare for writing this book, she traveled to Ireland again in 1980 armed with a tape recorder and a determination to learn about the country firsthand by meeting the people and visiting their homes and schools. Since her last visit, she has maintained a steady correspondence with many of her Irish friends, who have been valuable resources in gathering and validating primary source material.

Ms. Meyer has written several books for young people, including the highly acclaimed: *Ishi: The Story of an American Indian*, also published by Dillon Press. The author is a member of the Society of Children's Book Writers, the California Writer's Club, and the Burlingame Writer's Club. She lives with her two children in San Mateo.